W0035907

Advance Praise

This book indeed is a lucid rendition of some of the fundamentals of communication and networking. The power of communication is often repeated, but often ignored as well. Mr Mukerjee takes us back to these fundamentals in a nuanced manner with easy to read and digest, and relatable examples. Highly recommended for professionals across all levels.

Anant Deshpande, *Director Sales, Palo Alto Networks, India*

This book is a compelling read for all professionals from all walks of life. It captures the essence of effective communication and importance of building enduring relationships through the art of networking. We are seeing a paradigm shift in the way workplace productivity is measured and how positive and inclusive communication techniques add immense value to achieving team objectives in any organization. The author has brought his rich industry experience and training expertise to the fore while writing this masterpiece.

John Vincent, *Sr Presales Consultant,*
Kyriba Middle East FZ-LLC, Dubai

In today's over-communicated world where boundaries of communication between personal and professional lives have blurred, few listen and inter-generational communication has become a challenge, this book comes as a refreshing change in trying to convey the heart of the matter in a lucid and simple language, without being preachy or theoretical.

Dr Monica Khanna, *Director, K. J. Somaiya Institute of*
Management Studies & Research, Mumbai, India

Dr Hory Sankar Mukerjee's book *The Gift of the Gab: The Subtle Art of Communicating* offers incredible advice on how to communicate effectively. As a professional that has worked at the intersection of industry and academia for over two decades, Dr Mukerjee is uniquely placed to offer his pragmatic sagacity in a form that is both easy to understand and implement. I am certain that you will like the book as much as I did. It helps you understand how communication skills can be harnessed to build a strong personality and consequently a better personal brand.

Dr Praveen B. Malla, *Associate Director, Centre for Organization Development, Hyderabad, India*

I have known Hory for almost 15 years and if anyone can talk about communication, it is him. He is living embodiment of what is covered in this book. He is more of a listener, and when he talks it is nothing much except matter. This compilation of learnings and observations during his corporate tenure would be of immense value for anyone and everyone. I wish him best for this new book and future.

Sreejith Moolayil, *Co-founder, True Elements*

This book is written in an easy-to-read style and communicates important simple aspects of communication that we know at a subconscious level but fail or hesitate to practise well. It's a timely reminder and has well-chosen practical topics. I am sure that it will add value to all students of life. Congrats and wishing you all the best.

Jacqueline Pereira Mundkur, *Customer Experience Thought Leader and Sr Advisor (Retail/Consumer), Transaction Square Consultancy*

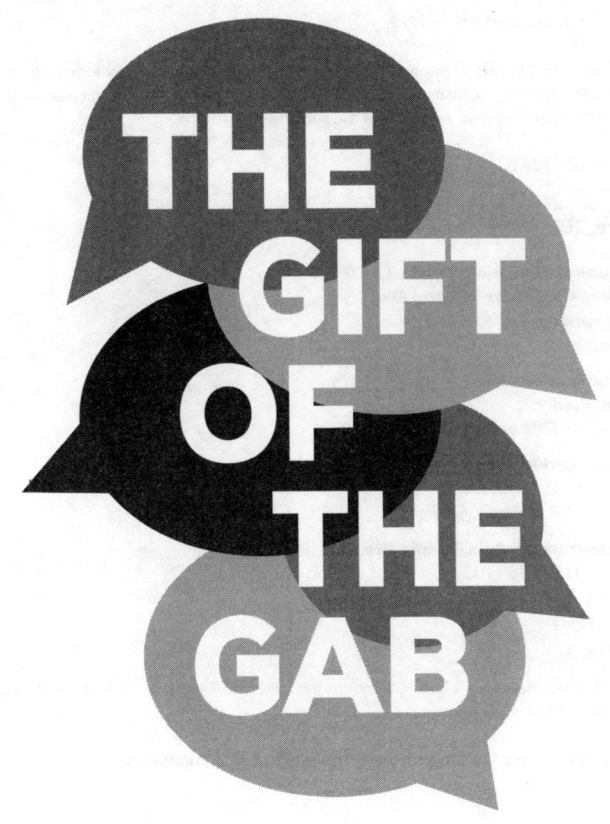

THE GIFT OF THE OF THE GAB

The Subtle Art of Communicating

HORY SANKAR MUKERJEE

Los Angeles | London | New Delhi
Singapore | Washington DC | Melbourne

First published in 2020 by

SAGE Publications India Pvt Ltd
B1/I-1 Mohan Cooperative Industrial Area
Mathura Road, New Delhi 110 044, India
www.sagepub.in

SAGE Publications Inc
2455 Teller Road
Thousand Oaks, California 91320, USA

SAGE Publications Ltd
1 Oliver's Yard, 55 City Road
London EC1Y 1SP, United Kingdom

SAGE Publications Asia-Pacific Pte Ltd
18 Cross Street #10-10/11/12
China Square Central
Singapore 048423

Published by Vivek Mehra for SAGE Publications India Pvt Ltd. Typeset in 10.5/13 pts Minion Pro by Fidus Design Pvt Ltd, Chandigarh.

Library of Congress Cataloging-in-Publication Data Available

ISBN: 978-93-5328-680-4 (PB)

SAGE Team: Manisha Mathews, Mahira Chadha, Ankit Verma and Rajinder Kaur

This book is dedicated to the Almighty
who has given me the strength to write,
my parents, Rima and Spandan—the
wonderful little kid

Thank you for choosing a SAGE product!
If you have any comment, observation or feedback,
I would like to personally hear from you.

Please write to me at **contactceo@sagepub.in**

Vivek Mehra, Managing Director and CEO, SAGE India.

Contents

Foreword

Hory and I were MBA batchmates at Symbiosis Institute of Management Studies (SIMS). It's through this association that I had the privilege of writing the foreword for Hory's first book, *Business Communication: Connecting at Work* and I'm absolutely delighted to be extended the same privilege again, and for the thrill of a hat-trick, I hope a third book is written.

Communication is a vital art form in everything we do. If applied effectively, it provides clarity of thought and purpose, creates trust and ensures productivity. Good communication is the bedrock of solid relationships as ineffective communication leads to a break down and this is largely as people talk at each other without listening, reflecting and communicating.

Communication is also a vastly underestimated life skill and with social media being ubiquitous, people are forgetting the subtle art of communicating. Being a vital ingredient in the recipe for change, through this book Hory is making a strong attempt to create awareness about good communication as people seldom stop to think about their style of communication. There is little difference in how people stand out when communicating and there lies an opportunity as the ones who have great skills have an extra edge.

In professional settings or a mid-large team, professional skills can only take you so far, it's good and strong communication skills that help us stand out from the crowd and get ahead.

I've been a communications professional for over 15 years with companies like Idea Cellular, BT, Facebook and Ola, and have lived and worked in India, Australia, UK and Singapore. The key skill that helped me navigate these years is strong communications skills which include verbal, non-verbal, social media and presentation skills, and honing the art of networking which is all about giving and listening. The ability to speak and write effectively is one of the most in-demand soft skills employers look for.

If one is willing to work on their communication skills, they can rapidly improve the quality of every part of life. Warren Buffett says, 'If you can't communicate and talk to other people and get across your ideas, you're giving up your potential.'

Carson Dalton,
Director, Ola Mobility Institute

Preface

We are in the corporate race and there is no way your work can be your differentiator. The work that you do or the sales targets or the operations that you manage are merely a 'hygiene' factor. It is the bare minimum essential for you to survive and the bread and butter that the company is expecting of you. All the people who are meeting their goals or exceeding in many cases are treated by their managers as 'expected' of them. So the real question that props up is, 'What else?' What is it that differentiates me from others? What is the X factor in 'me'?

The answer to this question lies in what we communicate, how we communicate and its effectiveness. There is no way for people to know unless you 'tell' it out to the world that this is what you have been doing. Managers today have a larger span of control. In some teams there could be as many as 10–30 people reporting. It is impossible for a manager to keep track of what you have been doing unless you explicitly talk about it. Your manager would also be armed with the inputs that he receives from the people you work with.

Being busy with our work-life and managing daily challenges do not allow us to focus on this most important skill of communicating. It is primarily due to a lack of self-awareness, our past habits and the pre-dominance of fear and anxiety to change. We need to initiate the changes, take baby steps in improving it. Communication is a learned habit. We need to practice and take corrective measures and excel.

It is time for professionals to bring about this change in how to listen with empathy, network for getting the work done and helping others, converse in a pleasant and productive way, communicate with honesty and openness with teams, write precisely and effectively, and present to touch the heart and soul of the listeners.

It is time to make the change. Whatever you do and whatever aspirations you nurture, you will not be able to make a mark unless you communicate like a professional. Just make it effective. Get through the hearts and the mind of your listeners and the world will synergize with you.

1 The Tortoise and the Hare Story: Retold

The art of communication is the language of leadership.

—James Humes

Once there was a hare and a tortoise, and they lived in a big jungle with other animals. The hare always bragged about how fast he could run. The tortoise, finally tired of the hare showing off, one day invited the hare for a race. The hare was happy as he could prove his point. The entire jungle came to see this race. All started placing their bets on the race as it was obvious that the odds were 1,000 to 1 for the hare.

The hare started off quick and looked back to see the tortoise coming slowly. He thought, 'What's wrong in taking some rest for a while?' The hare went off to sleep to take some rest. The tortoise, despite all his strength, was moving slowly. However, he gradually overtook the hare. When the tortoise was ending the race, the hare woke up, but it was too late. The tortoise ultimately won the race. The tortoise told the hare, 'Slow and steady wins the race!' But is this the complete truth?

As managers, we all love the hare at the beginning of the race. Hares are able to take care of themselves from few days after birth. They are fast runners. They can do things at incredible speed. As managers, employees who are fast and quick to produce results catch our attention quicker than those who are slow and steady. Our bias, unfortunately, is towards people who can produce results quickly, sometimes at the cost of sacrificing the quality. As a society, we are so focused on being faster and getting ahead that we forget that this will become our cause of failure in the long run, and if we are unable to evaluate ourselves or change our priorities, it will ultimately lead to our doomsday.

Rajat and Kinjal joined as management trainees sales in one of the largest insurance companies. Both of them came from the same business school and joined the same team of corporate sales. The responsibility given to both of them was the same. However, insurance as a product is difficult to sell, considering the lack of awareness among Indians and the dominance of a large public sector player. Everyone in the organization knew this. Anyone hired in this company was given a cooling-off period of six to eight months before they would be evaluated on their results. Kinjal proved to be different. She stood out and from the second month itself proved to be an absolute asset to the organization. She started cracking deals, so much so that even the existing employees started getting scared of her sales figures. Their manager went gaga over the performance of Kinjal. The manager was enjoying the limelight he got from the CEO because of Kinjal. As feared by all, she got her promotion in the next six months.

Rajat during this time was working slowly, building his network in the insurance industry and was learning how things worked. His performance was lacklustre and he was unable to produce great results but average. Their manager took the worst possible decision. He asked Rajat and a couple of the senior sales team members to report to Kinjal.

Over the next couple of quarters, Kinjal started off throwing her weight around. Although she put tremendous pressure on her reportees to perform, she put extra pressure on Rajat. Rajat was pinned down for everything and eventually a day came when he was forced to resign. Couple of the senior sales team members resigned with Rajat. The boss was still enjoying all of this as he was also due for his promotion. Eventually, in the next quarter, the boss got his promotion. Kinjal also threatened to leave the job unless her demands were met. She knew that the boss was heavily dependent on her success. However, as expected, she left the organization barely within two years of joining. Everyone (except for the CEO) pleaded her to stay back in the organization. What was the outcome? Along with the departure of Kinjal, the sales team was thoroughly demotivated, sales had plummeted and boss was clueless about his next step. Kinjal started working with a new organization and Rajat found out a job for himself, leaving a bad dream behind.

As managers, we loved Kinjal, but it ultimately led to failure. Had our focus been on Rajat as well, things probably would have turned out to be different.

So what happened to Rajat? Rajat left the job and sat with his friends, chatting about what could be done next. He did not have anything concrete in hand and he really did not know much of the city. He started building his network and applying for jobs. Things did not turn well initially. However, one of his customers from the earlier job met him by chance in a restaurant. Rajat was initially reluctant to take his referral, but the client offered help. He sent Rajat's resume to one of his friends and ultimately Rajat landed up in another job in the insurance industry. Rajat started working within a month of losing his job. He again started working on his competence and slowly grew up to be one of the most reputed and knowledgeable professionals in the area of insurance. His performance over the period was phenomenal.

Tortoises and hares exist in millions in the corporate world. There are so many of them around, doing their work relentlessly, that they bother more about 'giving' rather than 'taking' or vice versa. They act more as a facilitator rather than an inhibitor or vice versa. While cases like Rajat remain unnoticed by their managers, Kinjals outshine. Adam Grant in his book, *Give and Take* mentions that the conventional wisdom places the success of individuals to their motivation, ability and opportunity. However, Grant also makes a valid point about 'human interactions'—the fourth dimension of success. Do we claim value or do we contribute more than we receive in return?

Being a tortoise is not ugly and neither being a hare is evil. It is the person and his approach that make him go slow or fast, steady or inconsistent. Someone could be steady and ensure that he does his daily bit, while others are agile, wobbly and overconfident about their capabilities. There is nothing right or wrong in your approach if you are either the hare or the tortoise. However, it is important for you to understand that you can move from being the hare to the tortoise or vice versa, or a mix and match of both. You can be the most loved one, steady, fast, slow or agile. You can choose the words that describe you in the organization. However, it all depends on what you want to become or if you want to become someone at all. The choice is left on you, of how you want to be remembered the day you leave an organization. If you have chosen not to change and be the way you are, you are still correct and if you have chosen otherwise your decision is still right.

Being either is not wrong, but we all do crave for recognition or success of some sort. Even if we do not, we keep reminding ourselves about our aspirations and goals. Your success or recognition, and your aspirations and goals could be 'tangible' such as a promotion, salary or designation, or 'intangible' such as an appreciation or a pat on the back. Your aspiration could be something you want in the future. Something that you would have dreamt of, like writing a book or opening a café. However, whatever you aspire or achieve is possible only if you work towards it. Also, if you do not 'communicate' right with the right people about your aspirations or your goals, you will not achieve them. If you want to start a start up, you need to build the right network of people; if you want to rise up in the corporate ladder, you still need to do a lot communicating and building the right connections; if you intend to do the things that keep you going, you need to interact with people and if you intend to maintain status quo, you will still need to communicate. 'A mother feeds a crying baby' is something that we must remember and is extremely true in this chaotic corporate world. Therefore, to give your dreams and your aspirations the wings to fly, you must communicate 'right', irrespective of who you are.

Dianna Booher, for example, mentions that to become a leader five essential traits must be displayed by a person: Clear messaging, commanding presence, being credible, doing a great work and a core set of values whose impact will be felt by the people only in the way we communicate with them.[1]

Similarly, a book by Nancy Forbes and Basil Mahon on Faraday and Maxwell, talks about the genius Faraday.

> Perhaps the most revealing aspect is that he never demonstrated an experiment on stage, no matter how spectacular, unless he could also present the audience with the theory behind it. His scientific genius lay not simply in producing experimental results that had eluded everyone else *but in explaining them, too.*[2] [author's emphasis].

Therefore, be it science or business on two either sides of the spectrum, your skills to communicate will always matter. Your ability to communicate well, really has an impact.

When Bill Gates was talking in a 2009 TED conference, he released a swarm of mosquitoes to prove his point that only the poor should not suffer from malaria. He continued saying that mosquitoes have killed more people in history than all wars put together.

The impact of the right kind of communication can be tremendous. Look at how powerful non-verbal communication can be, when you do not speak with words. Your actions create a tremendous impact.

Vladimir Putin wrapped a shawl around Xi Jinping's wife while he was talking with Barack Obama. It was cold outside. Although this was okay for the Russian President and his people, it became a cause of worry for China for their conservative nature. They had to censor every off-colour joke that was being floated in the public domain in China.

---

[1] https://www.forbes.com/sites/womensmedia/2018/12/18/5-communication-skills-that-will-identify-you-as-a-leader/#66b419bdc8a5 (accessed on 29 April 2019).

[2] Nancy Forbes and Basil Mahon, *Faraday, Maxwell, and the Electromagnetic Field: How Two Men Revolutionized Physics* (New York, NY: Prometheus Books, 2014).

Communicating merely is not enough. It needs to be effective. As George Bernard Shaw puts it, 'The single biggest problem in communication is the illusion that it has taken place' should be treated with a great deal of seriousness. Excelling at work, being the most loved one, being steady, fast, slow or agile is not going to help you. What helps you is excellent and effective communication skills. Your ability to connect 'to' people and 'with' people is all that stands in between you and your aspirations.

HARE OR TORTOISE OR BOTH?

You cannot get away with the bell curve, neither choose your managers nor the work that you do. You will be graded either as a hare or a tortoise and you will need to carry out your tasks. You may or may not be recognized for your work, but you will relentlessly have to carry on with the work given to you. You will have to stick your neck down and complete your work. You must never lose sight of your aspirations, in any case, whether you are a hare or a tortoise. In either case, it is important at the same time that we 'communicate' to our managers, bosses, colleagues, customers and subordinates, effectively. Unless we do that, it is impossible for them to know, let even appreciate what we are doing and how it is increasingly difficult to execute things on the ground.

One of my friends, for example, was working in a large team. To create a difference, he used to send a mail to his manager every Friday after his boss had left office about the things that he had done, new initiatives and the impact that they had. I asked him about the difference that it made. He said, 'It really did not matter. It was just to keep him posted about what I was doing. Unless I do that, he will never know about my existence. There are about fifteen people who report to him and it is very unlikely that he really knows what I do.'

In the process, we must aim in building great relationships with people that make the journey more fruitful.

One of the banks that I worked with was headed by a very tough guy. He was extremely jovial, but turned extremely aggressive at times.

He was not the kind of guy that you would like to work with. However, he had a very good connect with the sales team. When he resigned from the organization and joined another, he offered almost all of them a new position in the new organization. While this is 'poaching' by industry standard terminology, this is also 'relationship building'.

Joseph Sommerville says, 'We take communication for granted because we do it so frequently, but it's actually a complex process.' We thoroughly underestimate the power of communication. Communication is not only about speaking. It is much more than that. It has a lot to do with how you write, how you present, how easily you connect to people, how you listen to people, how are your etiquettes, and how you manage difficult people and talk to them. It is not only about the written or the spoken words, it is also about the non-verbal cues that accompany them. That is what makes communication complex, really complex and an inevitable part of your work life.

So what do you want to become—the hare, the tortoise or the best of both the breeds? I would suggest you not to shift your gears, unless you really want to. Whatever you are, whatever your aspirations might be, ensure that you are great with your skill of communicating.

HOW DO WE COMMUNICATE?

Let us admit, we are not good at communication. CRICO Strategies reports that communication failures factored in 30 per cent of the cases of malpractice in healthcare, which included 1,744 deaths.[3]

We do not listen to people and are unwilling to take feedback, when given.

In one such case, a hotel had a policy of keeping away from bad feedbacks and reviews with a clause, 'Despite the fact that repeat

---

[3] https://www.managedcaremag.com/news/malpractice-report-finds-hospital-miscommunication-costs-17-billion (accessed on 30 April 2019).

customers and couples love our hotel, your friends and family may not. For every bad review left on any website, the group organizer will be charged a maximum £100 per review.' Although outrageous, one of the customers was charged for describing the hotel as 'rotten stinking hovel'. The money was directly charged to their credit cards without information to the customers. This is what was posted,

> We chose this hotel because it had "ample parking," car park was full so had to park across the road at another hotel. Couldn't believe the state of the room. The hot tap didn't work, when we reported it we were told they knew about it and it would be fixed in the morning (we were only there for one night.) The drawer fronts fell off when we opened the chest of drawers. Again, they knew about this and it was supposed to be dealt with in the morning. The kettle wouldn't work, were told you had to switch on the socket it was plugged into, also switch on another socket to make it work. This was because the whole place was rewired wrongly according to the member of staff who dealt with us, and they couldn't afford to have it put right. There were instructions on how to make a phone call, we would have had a job as there was no phone!! The wallpaper was peeling off the walls, the carpet was thin, dirty and stained. The bed was something else, it must have come out of the ark, the base was all scuffed and dirty and the springs in the mattress attacked you in the night. The curtains were tattered and filthy, there were polystyrene tiles on the ceiling which are a fire hazard.
>
> BREAKFAST…This was a joke and consisted of 1/2 cooked rasher of bacon, 1 "plastic" sausage, 1 egg, 1 hash brown and a spoonful of beans!! Oh, I nearly forgot, 2 slices of toast each, but no marmalade to put on them. Weak tea and coffee. YUMMY!! This place should be shut down, I don't know if they are ever inspected, but if so, I don't know how this place has passed!! If you are offered this place to stay for a fortnight for 10p, you are being robbed!! STAY AWAY!!!![4]

[4] https://www.bbc.com/news/uk-england-30111525 (accessed on 30 April 2019).

First, we spend a lot of time talking, rarely listening to people; and while we talk, we do not talk facts. We do not have sufficient inform-ation with us, which will help in the decision-making process. Similarly, when we write, we write in too many words or write about things that rarely matter to the people reading them.

Second, we do not plan our communication. We are thoroughly under-prepared about what we need to say or tell. We bury people with so much or so little information that they rarely understand the need of making such statements. Sometimes the information becomes so vague or irrelevant that people lose interest in what we intend to convey.

Project Management Institute's 2013 report suggests that US$135 million are at risk for every US$1 billion spent on a project. The research also suggests that 56 per cent of the projects are at risk due to ineffective communication. In spite of this, people agreed that focus is not on effective communication especially at a project level.[5]

Two common complaints from most of the clients are, 'Why did not you tell me this?' and 'Why did you not tell me that this was possible?'

Third, we do not communicate right. When it is time for us to speak up or keep silent, we do exactly the opposite. We do not speak or avoid speaking about bad news. We delay often indefinitely telling things that people should hear them out at the first instance and we avoid confronting people when we really need to.

A consulting company was working for a large multinational corpora-tion (MNC) on automating their sales process. The consulting company did a great job. The MNC had targeted to automate 50 per cent of their process, thereby saving time. In the final closure meeting, the MNC was discussing casually if they saw any scope in automating the process further. The project manager of the consulting company said,

---

[5] https://www.pmi.org/-/media/pmi/documents/public/pdf/learning/thought-leadership/pulse/the-essential-role-of-communications.pdf (accessed on 1 May 2019).

'The process can be made cent per cent automated.' The client was shocked to hear this. They said, 'Why didn't you tell this earlier? We could have easily got the budgets and automated it.'

Fourth, we do not build relationships with people, but merely deal with them or interact with them as transactions, as 'necessary conversations' at the workplace. We do not take utmost care to build a professional network both inside and outside the organization.

Pramod was my manager when I started my career. He was getting married after a year of my joining. One day while we were on a sales call, he went with his wedding card to one of our customers and invited him for his wedding. I asked him, 'So Pramod what is the logic behind inviting your customers for your wedding? It is highly unlikely that they are going to come. They are very busy.' What Pramod replied was amazing. He said, 'Although I work for this company, the client recognizes me as the face of this company. The company exists on paper, but I exist for them. It is also about building good relationships with people, irrespective of what you are doing or whether they are giving you business or not.' He proved to be right. Most of his customers, actually turned up for his wedding.

As a result of these, we realize that we have not been doing a good job at communicating. However most of our approaches to correct it are piecemeal. It is like the 'blind men' touching the elephant trying to describe how it looks like. The perspectives are different. Holistically if you need to improve, you will need to work on all the skills. These lifelong skills and you will need to continuously work towards them.

COMMUNICATION SETS THE FLOOR

The two most popular questions that I have been asked on Quora (a social forum for gaining and sharing knowledge) are first, 'How do I improve my communication skills?' and second, 'I have x number of days to improve my skills. How should I go about doing this?'

Unfortunately, there is no answer to the second question. It is like predicting the stock markets. There is no time to success or failure, but there is endless time for learning the skills again and again. Communication cannot be perfected in a day or a month. It takes years to do it. Sometimes people would succeed, sometimes they won't. The failure however won't come for those who do not try or leave it in between. They would be the ones who set goals, try to improve but rarely operationalize things. Improving their ability to communicate is next to impossible. It requires constant self-monitoring and a self-conscious effort to improve with lots of practice. So the three pillars for you to do this magic are: First to put the efforts in the right direction, second to monitor yourself and the third to keep practicing. Along with this you need friends such as Hermione and Ron (reference *Harry Potter*) who would tell you what went wrong or right.

The first question however is the easiest. The answer is to practice. There are no shortcuts, guides and rules. You can have a mentor who can guide you, or people whom you listen to be inspired or you aspire to become. The journey to become the best however lies with you. You will have a certain set of frameworks, some best practices and some tips shared with you. You will need to use them, mix up your experience, benchmark the best and keep improving yourself. However, do not be shy to talk or communicate any time. Reflect on what you did right or wrong. A diary to keep a note helps.

Brijesh was my senior at a hotel management school. He came from a rural background and was trained at one of the remotest of schools in India. His language was not great, could not speak and was extremely uncomfortable talking to people around. He used to fumble. However, communication is a very important aspect in the hospitality industry. After college we lost touch. Fifteen years later, he connected with me on LinkedIn. He wanted to talk to me about something. We shared our numbers and he called me. I was amazed when he introduced himself. I was in an awe, when I heard him speak. He was not the same Brijesh. He had transformed himself into something wonderful.

His communication was exemplary. No doubt he had become the head of marketing for one of the largest global hotel chains.

The point is simpler. It takes TIME.

WHAT ABOUT MANAGERS?

It's important to make sure that we're talking with each other in a way that heals, not in a way that wounds.

—Barack Obama

Just as you evaluate your hares and tortoises, you also get your unfair share of evaluation. You cannot crib now on being unfair. However, the challenges for you are even bigger. You have a team of people and your success is ultimately dependent on them. Your ability to communicate with them and their ability to communicate amongst themselves to get the work done are extremely critical. Therefore, the skill set of being able to manage a great team, a team which is diverse in every sense, and an ability to persuade them to do something are even greater challenges for you. You can add necessary frills to this like a virtual team or a VUCA environment as they talk about it frequently today.

The hare and the tortoise story did not end there. The hare was shocked at his defeat, however realized his mistake. They became friends and finally decided that they would work together forever. The king of the jungle got inspired with this race and decided to do this for all the animals. This time however in a different territory. He gave a map and asked all of them to run. After running for some time, they reached a river. The tortoise with his ability to swim agreed to carry the hare on his back. The hare responded back after crossing the river. It took the tortoise on his back and ran the last half of the race and they reached the finishing line way before the others.

As a manager, I believe that we are biased towards hares than tortoises. However, realize that they have their own set of capabilities, strengths and weaknesses. Labelling a person as a hare or a tortoise is not right or being equal and fair. Some days consistency would out-weigh the speed and other days it would be vice versa. As a manger, therefore your aim should to be able to persuade them effectively to complete a task with honest, open and trustworthy communication. Realize that they have their own potential to run, and to get the best from a team, you must overcome your biases. As Anne Morrow Lindbergh puts it, 'Good communication is as stimulating as black coffee, and just as hard to sleep after.'

2 Hearing the Unsaid

*All credibility, all good conscience, all evidence of truth
come only from the senses.*

—Friedrich Nietzsche

As Peter F. Drucker once said, "The most important thing in communication is hearing what isn't said."

Contrary to popular belief, the factor that forms the greatest impression is not words but the non-verbal cues we pick up via body language, eye contact and voice inflection. The first impression through unspoken words is made in just one-sixth of a second. These kinds of subtle communications deliver more information about the intent of the speaker than the words he/she uses when speaking.

NON-VERBAL CUES

Imagine a situation when your team leader comes to your cubicle, drops a bundle of files and asks you to take a look and send him a report. You are surprised by his behaviour as he had never behaved like this earlier. When you ask him, he says, 'It's ok', turns his back and walks away.

You are in a dilemma and do not understand which one to trust: his words, his actions or his earlier image that you had about him. These are the non-verbal cues or signals beyond words and they can be more powerful in conveying meaning than spoken words. The cues include what you wear, your body language, your expressions, way of saying, your voice and the space around you.

Talking or conversations remain our primary form of communication, used primarily for conveying data or a message. When you hear someone talk, our tendency is to spend a lot of our time in listening and deriving a meaning of what is being said, but what we do not focus on is the 'body language' or the 'non-verbal cues'. These become areas of least interest or focus.

Have you experienced situations when your manager promised you something for your career prospects, but did not keep up? Or a situation when your customer told you that he would buy it from you, but denied later or when your team members said that they support you in your decision only to back out later or a unanimous 'yes' from the sales team, only backing out later from their commitments. These are not uncommon, but had you spent some time reading their non-verbal cues you would have gotten a feel of what they had 'said' versus what they had actually meant. Professor Albert Mehrabian, from UCLA, did his studies in the area of non-verbal communication and proposed a '7%–38%–55% rule' for communication. The first 7 per cent accounted for the impact of words, 38 per cent on the tone of voice with which a person is speaking and 55 per cent to the body language.

Look at the characters of Sir Charles Spencer Chaplin or Charlie Chaplin and Rowan Atkinson or Mr Bean. Both these people used slapstick, mime, and bold, exaggerated movements, facial expressions and actions for their audience to stay glued. Even in the days of silent films, Chaplin was able to convey using expressions. Mr Bean is equally great in an age when spoken words matter the most. Most of his communication is rarely verbal, and he conveys his words through the use of physical actions, facial expressions and body movements. So a successful TV series or movies relevant even today has been created 'just' with the power of symbols, actions and expressions.

Ignoring the non-verbal cues can never be an alternative for a great manager or a leader. Just as you tend to focus on the words, equal or even more focus should be on the words that are unspoken. They convey attitude, emotions, moods and much more than what the speaker might want to reveal.

Rajat is a senior level executive. Whenever he is called in front of an audience, he always prefers to talk behind a podium. He takes the support of the podium and a piece of paper on which he scripts down everything he has to say. He scratches his head often, rubs his nose, drinks at least two glasses of water, and sometimes moves from behind the podium to the centre of the stage and again comes back to the podium. However, when he is facing the audience, his hands are folded and the legs are positioned as a scissor.

All of these are examples of lack of self-confidence, insecurity and conviction. We all make judgements about people and so do others about us. It is important that we make a lasting impression and communicate what we desire or what we intend to do. In both these cases, while spoken words come much later, how we groom ourselves, and how we convey using our gestures, body language and etiquettes evaluate us as a person. So when you are being judged or you are judging someone, you will do that on the basis of these three major components: first is the attire, second is the body language and third is the etiquette. This will significantly impact your success at the workplace. Therefore, when you rely only on the words, you rely only on the words, but you will only be able to dig deeper inside a person when you look holistically at a person with these perspectives. While projecting yourself as a good leader or a team player, you need to demonstrate confidence, positivity and professionalism. These can only be gathered from the non-verbal signs, what you wear and how you present yourself to the world around you. It becomes imperative for employers, employees, superiors and subordinates to understand this important aspect of communication.

NEVER UNDERESTIMATE THE POWER OF ATTIRE

Clothes make the man. Naked people have little or no influence on society.

—Mark Twain

Office attire has changed over the years. While organizations earlier were more formal with the employee attire, now the trend is business casual. It is difficult to define what business casuals is because it varies across geographies, however some organizations define it and others leave it on their employees to decide.

Look out for specific attire related note or policy that your organization may be having. Ensure that you follow it, which not only makes you get at par with your organizational requirements but also projects a good image.

A CEO was on a visit to his top client. While they were talking about 'what can be done' and their 'feedback', the customers had no issues with the deliverables. However, a thing that was brought to the notice of the CEO was the 'dress code' that the employees followed. 'While your guys are brilliant, I have issues with what they wear. Our company is traditionally very conservative and we expect that our vendors working within our premises follow the dress code that has been prescribed. Even after sensitizing them about the issue, they really do not seem to care. Can you please pass on the message to them?' The CEO took their suggestion and directed HR to formulate a dress code policy for the employees. Easier said than done, a lot of resistance was from the employees citing various reasons. Implementing a policy globally across the organization was difficult as the company had over a million employees with people from different cultural backgrounds.

'Does attire influence others?' and 'Does it influence you as a person?' are perhaps the two biggest questions. Recent scientific experiments conducted on the attire that you wear seem to suggest that it does influence you as well as others. Dr Jennifer Baumgartner wrote a book titled, *You Are What You Wear: What Your Clothes Reveal about You* in which she explains that psychology determines the clothing choice of a person. In another experiment by Professor Karen Pine from the University of Hertfordshire, she asked her students to put on a Superman t-shirt. After wearing it, the students rated themselves as physically stronger, could lift more weight and were more likeable than other students. Professor Pine rightly puts, 'Not only that we are what we wear, but that we become what we wear.'

Bharat always loved his sporty look and was known for wearing offbeat clothing. He chose to work in sales after his graduation and joined a media company. While the company did not have a dress code, employees were expected to wear formals till Thursday and business casual on Friday. Bharat took the 'business casual' too casually. One Friday morning, he entered the office wearing a floral shirt with red pants. The sales manager was talking with some of his managers and while Bharat was entering, the sales manager stopped him. The first question directed to Bharat was, 'Don't you have a sales call today?' Bharat nods affirmative. The sales manager shook his head in dismay and then smiled at Bharat and said, 'I admire the sales person who sold you this shirt.' Bharat smiled and went away. Later in the evening, HR called Bharat for a meeting and educated him about professional dressing.

Everything that you are wearing has a deep and an inherent meaning. It may be symbolic, but holds true. Do they signify that you feel different every time you wear them? Research suggests so. The attire that you carry has a strong influence on you as well as others. Dressing in a way can lift you up from a current state and since it has the power to influence 'how' you want to feel, use it to your benefit. Another advice from Dr Jennifer Baumgartner is, 'There is no style that can make a person look successful or unsuccessful. However, the worst form of attire is the one which tries to undo, hide or ignore where or who you are.'

In business, you should be ready to dress according to the occasion. The first, of course, is to understand what you would want yourself to be projected as. For example, you would need to wear something different in a panel or a discussion, a meeting with your clients or at work daily. The second course is to try and get inspired from what people wear. While it is not suggested to be a copycat, you can always be inspired by how people dress. Overhaul your wardrobe every 2–3 years and eliminate things wisely. Ensure that you keep your age, relative hierarchy in your organization, occasion and your perceived image that you would want to project in mind before deciding your attire. The third is to understand what you shop for. While shopping ensures that you are aware of the gaps in your wardrobe, assess what you already have. Ensure that you are aware of what is available in your wardrobe and buy things that add to your personal collection of grooming. Avoid a fascination towards a colour or design. Along with your garments, spend time with some of the accessories that you wear. One of the easiest ways is to experiment with what you wear and notice the reactions of people around you.

A group of senior managers were on a client visit after a recently concluded consulting project. The client was very impressed with the work done and the managers were upbeat about future business coming from the assignment. After dinner, the client pointed out, 'While your guys are extremely great at their work, but please ask them to change their socks frequently. I think you all pay your employees well.'

Your daily look at the workplace is of importance. While your organization may or may not define business casual, ensure that you are well groomed at the office. Casuals do not mean showing off skin, nor should they impact your productivity or that of the others. Plan your week in advance. Every weekend spend some time in getting your attire ready for the week. If you do this, it will leave you enough time not to hurry through every morning worrying about what to wear. Keep your accessories in order, along with your attire. In case you are new to an organization, spend some days observing what others wear.

A SMILE COSTS NOTHING

Smile, it is the key that fits the lock of everybody's heart.

—Anthony J. D'Angelo

Jyoti had been working with us for some years. She decided to move on after her marriage. On the last day, we organized a farewell. While others were giving their feedback about Jyoti, her manager was quiet. At the end, the manager was asked to say a few things about her. This is what he had to say, 'There are a few people I have seen in my life smiling all throughout the day. It was a big stress buster for me. I used to often look up to her smile to gather some energy while I used to get bogged down with work. I have never seen her frown despite heavy workload and this is what I like about her. If I miss Jyoti after she has left this company, it will be because of her wonderful and everlasting smile on her face.'

Body language forms an essential component of the non-verbal cues, and the first is the smile. As an old adage goes, 'A smile costs nothing', you in business should be seen portraying a genuine and an honest smile. Smiling is universal in nature and enjoyable. When you smile at people, you get it back in reciprocation. Understand that while smiles can be genuine, it is possible to fake a smile. Professor Ruth Campbell, from University College London, finds that smiling has a mimicking action. This is because of a 'mirror neuron' that triggers the instant mirroring reaction. Smiling, therefore, has an important role to play. Even if you do not feel great about smiling back at a person, start now. When you are happy, the easiest way to spread the happiness is to smile. Another important aspect of smiling is the 'mood-lift' that you get when you smile in return. It also portrays a very positive image about you as a person and radiates positive energy around. You may express nervousness or unfriendliness when you do not smile or put on a fake one, that is, when you really do not feel it is important. So smile genuinely and frequently.

I love signings and having eye contact with a reader who already knows my soul.

—Paulo Coelho

You are at an alumni meet and you are meeting your friend after a long time. Just as you both started initiating a talk, you notice your friend's eyes have started wondering around the room. You wonder if he is seriously interested in talking to you. While you feel dejected that he has not given you his attention, you are also willing to let go of him as he seems disinterested. Is it that he is unwilling to listen or is he listening, just without his eyes looking at you? You are now in a real dilemma.

Eye contact is an essential part of a conversation and a very important non-verbal cue. The eyes are the most revealing and accurate predictors because you cannot control them. The eyes have a powerful role to play. We express our happiness, surprise, pleasure, dislike, suspicion with our eyes. For example, a trainer/teacher looks at the eyes of his audience to understand their 'pulse'. A great listener will always maintain an eye contact with the person who is talking. A mutual interest is generated and developed as a result of an eye contact. If you want to be perceived by the other person as sincere and honest, maintain the contact. Eye contact also gives you a cue when the other person is not listening. If you find someone you are talking to focusing on other things and not on your eyes, it is time to bid goodbye. He is simply not listening to you. You also lose your trustworthiness and credibility. For any presentations, therefore ensure that you maintain the eye contact. You connect with your audiences better. Eye contact does not mean domination in any form. It is associated with rudeness when done wrongly, especially when a person is staring at you.

Another yet effective way to build rapport with a person is to look in between the eyes and the forehead. This is the best zone to focus on. If you want a person to be stopped, just focus in between their eyes. Remain silent for some time. In case you want to walk out of any situation, the easiest way to do is to break eye contact. Your starting to look around is a good signal that you want to break away from the conversation. However, avoiding eyes would also mean that you could be acting submissively or you do not intend to reciprocate or you are getting uncomfortable with the talking that is happening. Eyes are difficult to control and in all ways they become the easiest measure to understand a person's body language. So if you are trying to understand someone, look at his eyes along with his other gestures.

YOUR FACE SAYS IT ALL

While giving a job interview or engaging at a networking event, the facial expressions will convey what is going on within a person. In essence, one's face says much more than one can think, and very often more than what one can orally convey.

Facial expressions are the second most recognizable non-verbal cue after eye contact. In this era of emojis, even our smart phones have facial expressions. Whatever is said versus what the face expresses is a unique way to understand a person. It is perhaps very difficult to hide the emotional state of a person against the reflection on our face. Therefore, the more expressive your face is, the easier it is for people to connect.

Andre Agassi and Boris Becker were legendary tennis players. However, when Agassi took to the court, he could not beat Becker in 1988 and 1989. Becker scored a hat-trick during these two years. Agassi wanted to break the winning streak of Becker, and to do that, he kept on watching the videos of Becker playing. He noticed one surprising thing when he repeatedly watched Becker serving. Just before Becker served the ball, he would stick his tongue out. If it went to the left of his mouth, he was serving towards the tramlines and if it remained in the middle the ball would be placed centrally. Agassi with his new discovery turned the matches around. In the following meetings on the court, Becker could win only one out of the eleven times they met, before he retired in 1999. Agassi, later said, 'The hardest part wasn't returning his serve, but not letting him know that I knew this.'[1]

It has been found out that people from different cultures show the same facial expressions for 'six' basic emotions (anger, disgust, fear, happiness, sadness and surprise).

---

[1] https://timesofindia.indiatimes.com/blogs/O-zone/agassis-secret-weapon-can-be-yours-too/ (accessed on October 2019).

More than talking, it is important to express, and facial expressions convey a lot more than what words necessarily would do for you. You tend to smile when a toddler walks around the house or when a friend walks up to you, and bear a frown when you incidentally meet someone you did not want to. These are all different expressions that you have. An out-of-the-turn promotion, a surprising bonus, unhappiness with team performance, fear of being reprimanded during recession and a new task being assigned to you will instill different kinds of response on your face. While you are open and positive, your face expresses happiness and incisiveness when you are 'appearing to be happy'. These facial expressions coupled with the eyes, gestures, body movements and your voice work wonders.

Your facial expressions will automatically reflect what you intend to express. You really do not need to put much effort unless you are trying to fake it. But keep in mind that faking for a longer time is difficult. As someone who is observing the facial expressions of his manager, colleague or peers, ensure that you read the facial expressions right. While happiness is easiest to read, the sadness of a person can be read from a dull face. A person would probably look more introvert and down in such situations. If a person gets surprised, their eyes widen while their mouths open up, and nod in cases of interest or agreement.

BREAKING BARRIERS WITH THE POWER OF GESTURES

The gesture of your *hands* is very powerful and indeed speaks a lot like your eyes and your face. It resonates what you are saying, especially when you are trying to emphasize on a particular aspect or a word. The first imminent message conveyed when your hand is in the pockets is that you are trying to demonstrate superiority or trying to lie. This sign is also used for non-participation or lack of willingness. Another common sign of lying is to hide your hands behind your back. This is a very common sign that kids have especially when they are unwilling to talk or are trying to hide things. Another common signal that people have is to keep their hands folded, which is seen as a gesture of dominance or restraint or closeness. You are either trying to position yourself as a dominating person or you are closing yourself from the ideas of others. Keeping the hands clasped demonstrates nervousness, such as while watching the finals of a match or a thriller. Never stand with folded arms or with your hands in your pockets just because you find it comfortable. These are wrong messages that you send. The best way is to keep it sideways with open palms facing downwards, while you talk to the other person or use your hands to express yourself and support the words that you speak. If you want to understand if a person is giving the right reason to reject or accept, take a close look at his palms. If he opens and shows his palm, he is probably being honest.

Handshakes are the best way to express your dominance or submission to the other person. You will be sending out a welcome message with your handshake. While there are various types of handshakes, ensure that you are not giving a bone-crushing handshake. People avoid shaking their hands with bone crushers. While some do it willingly, some demonstrate superiority using a bone crusher. A limped, cold, or touching the fingertip handshake is also unacceptable in business context as one needs to show a sign of sincerity or willingness or connectedness. The right way to shake your hand is when you give a firm shake with the same amount of pressure the other person gives and palm is in a vertical position, which is a sign of mutual trust. Coming too close to shake hands or embracing after shaking hands, using double hands for the first meeting or jerking the hands is a no-no during business handshakes. Extending to shake hands with a woman is a no-no in certain cultures, especially the Middle East. Always remember that if you are younger than the other person or if you have come uninvited like a sales cold call, never extend your hands first. The other person may not be comfortable to shake their hands, which brings in a degree of discomfort.

Arms demonstrate your feelings and your attitude when you open or close them. Approaching a person with an open arm versus a closed one demonstrates your feelings for the person. While you may want to keep them open in some situations, keep them closed for some, especially when you are planning to move out from a conversation. Another common sign is a person with crossed arms across their chests. While this is more uncommon in women, except for when they are trying to feel more secure, men demonstrate this more often. Crossed arms act as a shield of defensiveness or uneasiness in a particular situation. If the palms are open with open arms, they signal openness. Many times people close their arms or hug them with their arms, simply because they find it comfortable, especially when they are listening. Read it with caution.

Thumbs up is a sign which denotes an agreement with the other person. However, thumbs often represent superiority over the other person. In Greece, however, this denotes similar to the middle finger of the American. Similarly, when you want to demonstrate superiority, you may have your thumb out of the pocket. Thumbs are generally used with other non-verbal cues.

The *legs* are the farthest from your brains and we rarely focus on what is happening with our legs. We take them for granted and often do not put a keen watch of the non-verbal cues. The first, of course, is how we walk and the most confident way of all is to keep the arms marching along with the legs, at a comfortable pace. Walking demonstrates a sign of your attitude. Keeping hands in the pocket while walking expresses dominance or high-headedness. Like your arms, the openness and the closedness of your legs also demonstrate similar behaviour. If you keep your legs crossed, you are appearing as a closed person or you are closing your thoughts and views. While standing, some people prefer to stand straight with both their feet together, while some keep them at a distance and arms on their hips. While the former is mostly done by women, it denotes 'silence'. Cross-legged sitting may indicate superiority over the others. They try to dominate others.

THE SPACE AROUND YOU

The impact of space around us can be understood by just looking at our behaviour in elevators. When you start riding inside an elevator, people tend to stand with some gap unless they know someone very well. When the elevator starts filling up, people start moving around or stepping back and forth to keep some distance from others. These adjustments keep on happening until there is no space left in the elevator. You keep coming closer to the people whom you know well or at least have seen or met. After the elevator is full and it stops at a certain floor, people standing outside refuse to get in unless they find sufficient space for themselves. People inside the elevator do not talk or smile, avoid eye contact, get engrossed with their mobile/ newspaper, look at the ceiling of the lift or at the display board of the floors crossing and appear poker faced or neutral. This is how the space around you works. Or, for example, if you have a colleague who comes very close to you while talking, you tend to walk back or shift. This is again because they would have invaded your personal space. The most important thing about personal space is that you have the ability to control how you position yourself against a person. Your frame of mind changes completely with the change of space. A person automatically responds to the invasion of his space. He could be turning around, walking away or give himself a gap when he is invaded.

There are four zones or spaces around us: intimate, personal, social and public. Intimate is the space up to a feet and half around you, personal is the space up to 5 feet, social is about 12 feet and anything beyond that is public. So more a person moves from public to a personal zone, you feel threatened unless you know the person well. The intimate and personal space is for people whom you know very closely and the social and personal space are for your friends and the people at large. For example, you would feel threatened by someone who is asking for a direction, standing far away from you in the public space.

Humans do not like invasion of their personal space and if you have not invited a person or you do not know them, you generally show signs of disturbance. Putting objects in between, turning around, walking away and not making an eye contact are signs that you are scared of the invasion of your personal space. In most of the circum-stances, people avoid this invasion, but in certain cases it cannot be avoided. The rule of thumb is to stay away from the intimate zone when you do not know a person and in business occasions avoid the intimate zone as much as possible. Stay around in the personal zone as much as you can unless the person in front asks you or signals his acceptance to move into the intimate zone. Each person has their own territory or sub-territory. For example, you feel more comfortable when you are sitting with your team members than moving into other departments or space.

READING THE SIGNS

Reading the non-verbal cues is essential as the words that one speaks comprise only data and facts. They do not tell the mental position of the person, their attitudes or the feelings associated with what the person is trying to say. So as someone who is listening, you should attempt to understand them, which will tell about their mental condition. While some of these conditions come naturally to us, a person speaking will be unable to fake their non-verbal cues for long. However, some caution before you start reading a person. The first, of course, is to read it in context of the subject. For example, it has been a long day at office and you are sitting with your heads lying back, arms supporting them and looking at the ceiling. While this may signify disinterest in other situations, it could also mean that you are tired at the end of the day. This leads us to the second rule of reading the non-verbal cues, that is, reading the signals in totality. Observe for some time before you actually start reading a person and derive a meaning. Unless you get sufficient signs to affirmatively confirm, you should never interpret. The third rule is the rule of the culture. While some hand symbols may be okay in your country, they may be not in other parts of the world. Similarly, a person who has been raised in an urban background, will exhibit a different behaviour and expression than someone who comes from a semi-urban or rural background. While you will be exposing yourself to different people across the globe exhibiting different behaviour, ensure that you respect and appreciate them for the differences.

While listening to the content of the speaker is important, it may be very difficult for you to focus on the non-verbal cues as we do not read it as a natural practice. However, the best way to practice is to focus on discussions in which you would focus only on the non-verbal aspects of communication. This inculcates a habit to read the non-verbal cues.

> By a man's finger-nails, by his coat-sleeve, by his boots, by his trouser-knees, by the callosities of his forefinger and thumb, by his expression, by his shirt-cuff—by each of these things, a man's calling is plainly revealed. That all united should fail to enlighten the competent inquirer in any case is almost inconceivable.[2]

LEVERAGING YOUR NON-VERBAL COMMUNICATION

You may want to use the non-verbal cues to your benefit. You can surprisingly increase your collaboration, confidence, participation and positive feelings by exhibiting positive non-verbal cues. To *collaborate* effectively, remove any physical barrier that may come in between the people, for example, a board or podium or coffee cup, or to connect with people better, it is suggested that you shake your hands in the first meeting. A problem that comes up for trainers/people chairing the meetings is to increase the level of *participation*. The easiest way to do that is by building eye contact. You can also go to the middle of the room or walk around the room to increase the level of participation. To evoke *positive feelings*, the easiest way is to smile. When you smile at someone, there is an automatic positive response from the other person. Other ways to do it are to listen with empathy or acknowledge if you are listening to someone.

ETIQUETTES MATTER

The annual sales meeting is over and you are lucky to have your CEO this year along with you. He has invited the entire team of sales people for a cocktail dinner. Some of the new sales hires who have joined the company recently form a small group, ignoring the rest of crowd. They are busy with their drinks and snacks while the programs were on. The senior managers try to break the ice, however

---

[2] Arthur Conan Doyle, *Sherlock Homes: A Study in Scarlet*

get a cold shoulder from them. Finally, at the end of the evening, some of them get drunk turning the dinner into a mess. Few of the folks fight with the stewards of the hotel hurling abuses at one another. The CEO quickly leaves the scene asking one of the senior managers to handle it.

'Etiquette is not some rigid code of manners, it's simply how persons' lives touch one another', this is how Emily Post, best-selling author and founder of the Emily Post Institute and a world authority on etiquette defines it. This subject however has been in discussion for two centuries now, with the first recorded usage by Philip Stanhope, who was the 4th Earl of Chesterfield. He had written over 400 letters to his son in between 1737 and 1768 on various subjects, published in 1774. In these letters, Stanhope attempted to differentiate manners from morality, suggesting that etiquette was important for social advancement.[3]

In a business context, the rise of incivility or rudeness at work is on the rise. A research work done by Christine Porath and Christine Pearson[4] speaks about rising incivility and its consequences at the workplace. Nightly-eight per cent employees reported to have experienced incivility. The impact post the incidents was people worrying about the incident, losing their commitment to work, taking out frustrations on others, leaving their job and many others intentionally decreasing their efforts they put at work.

It therefore becomes important to be a good role model for your peers and subordinates and manage yourself better.

The workplace etiquette becomes critical for everyone, whether it is managers, leaders, subordinates or peers. Your behaviour and interaction with others has an impact on one another, on yourself, your relationship and commitment with others in business, and

---

[3] https://en.wikipedia.org/wiki/Philip_Stanhope,_4th_Earl_of_Chesterfield (accessed on 26 May 2019).

[4] Christine Porath and Christine Pearson, 'The Price of Incivility,' *Harvard Business Review*, (January–February 2013), https://hbr.org/2013/01/the-price-of-incivility (accessed on 26 May 2019).

therefore, we must keep the etiquette in mind. Etiquettes are a very sensitive issue in business and there are very good chances that you may lose business or reputation because of lack of it. Imagine someone walking to your office, smoking a 'cigarette'. You might not get a very professional image of the person or the company which he represents and you would resist doing business with him. Good etiquettes will make others notice you, but poor ones can destroy your image badly. Etiquettes define your personal brand.

Here are some of things that you must practice at the workplace.

Akshata always had a grudge against her manager. She used to complain about him and whenever there was any discussion, she would invariably speak about him and how he troubled her with stuff. However, her manager was quite considerate and helpful. This continued so much that people used to walk away from her whenever she started speaking about her manager. After a year had passed on like this, Akshata got into a personal trouble. Her mother needed some money for an emergency operation. The moment Akshata' s manager came to know about this, he went out of his way to help her. He also asked his colleagues to contribute. The operation was successfully done and her mother was back at home. Akshata was again back to her usual self after the appraisal, comfortably forgetting about his help. When she was again discussing this with his colleagues on how rude and adamant her manager was, one of her colleagues told her that they envy her of having such a manager and it was she who did not realize how good a person he was. They turned around Akshata realizing that she was not worthy of being a colleague.

As an employee, you must appreciate and respect your company culture. Culture is shared values, beliefs, attitudes and working norms. Understand and respect the nature of the organization and its people, hierarchies, addressing of its people and the working environment of the company. Help your colleagues in any way you can, especially new hires and people struggling at work. Give compliments to your colleagues for any good work that they have done. A handwritten note goes way beyond an electronic note. Help without overburdening yourself or expecting future favours. 'Save the faces of your colleagues' and avoid passing the buck, especially when there is a problem or escalation. Give people around you an open and comfortable environment to interact. Respect company confidentiality. Do not give out information or break the principles or be on the wrong side of the fence.

You will have personal differences with your organization or your manager, but you must act loyal in front of your stakeholders and clients. Avoid criticizing your own company and people. If you feel that things are not right or something bothers you, quit. Empathize with your people and protect them. Avoid gossips of any kind, especially at coffee breaks and water coolers. They are unproductive and derogatory. Leaving office for personal work for long hours, surfing the net and using the office resources for personal use must be avoided. Let your poor planning and erratic behaviour not be a cause of hardship for others. It could result into a very pathetic work culture. Humour which hurts others especially if they are gender-, region-, or religious-based are best avoided. Advising people is to be avoided unless specifically asked for. Issues such as divorces, pregnancy, health issues, death, marriage, engagements and firing are sensitive and touchy. Never advise people in such cases.

Resolve conflicts with professionalism. Avoid personal confrontation or taking revenge for a previous workplace conflict. Any conflicts should be solved out in closed rooms and never in front of your colleagues. Avoid biased use of words such as 'handicapped', and 'deaf and dumb', although we often mention 'physically challenged' as a replacement to the biased language while speaking or writing.

Give 100 per cent to your people and work. Avoid eating at the desk (especially if the dining hall or cafeteria is small), shutting the door on people, speaking loudly in open spaces, eating the tiffin of others, using speaker phone when people are working around or gossiping with people around you. Other etiquette issues could be talking in the toilet and using office devices and facilities. Please recognize the protocols of your office and adhere to them. Spend couple of days observing people when you are moving to a new organization or office or department.

Approach your boss with an open mind, take new initiatives and avoid discussing 'him' or confronting him directly and complaining in general. A lot of these are dependent on how his attitude is, and therefore, you should be wise enough to understand what he likes and dislikes. Understand when to respond to criticism from your boss. If some things can be left off, you rather should. Relationships at office are also a part of etiquette.

Relationships at office are a sensitive subject, and one should avoid having one. It leads to a lot of speculation and gossips, especially issues of favouritism, bias and taking undue advantage crop up. If the relationship turns sour, it could lead up to cases of harassment and later termination. Ensure that you do not jeopardize your career. Avoid misusing your position, degree or grade to give or receive a favour. Office politics must better be avoided. The best way is to walk out of a discussion or not contribute to a discussion in such circumstances.

If you want to create a difference to yourself and your personal brand, use a three-pronged approach. First focus on your attire. Dress well for every occasion. You must carry yourself extremely well for every day and occasion at the office. Second focus on your non-verbal cues. Ensure that you approach with an open mind and are honest in what you say or act. The third is taking care of your etiquette. Your etiquette will give you the edge over others.

BIBLIOGRAPHY

1. Kathleen Bogart, 'Facial Expressions Are Key to First Impressions. What Does that Mean for People with Facial Paralysis?', *The Conversation*, 27 May 2016, https://theconversation.com/facial-expressions-are-key-to-first-impressions-what-does-that-mean-for-people-with-facial-paralysis-59359 (accessed on 26 May 2019).

2. Allan Pease and Barbara Pease, *The Definitive Book of Body Language* (Australia: Pease International, 2004).

3. Elizabeth Kuhnke, *Body Language for Dummies* (UK: John Wiley & Sons, 2007).

3 The Power of Networking

WHAT IS NETWORKING?

Networking has been cited as the number one unwritten rule of success in business. Who you know really impacts what you know.

—Sallie Krawcheck

Ravi published his first book in 2013 and ever since has been travelling across the country talking to students and the faculty community. After every meeting he ensures that he shares his contact details and LinkedIn profile with them. He leaves them with a proposition that they can get in touch with him for help or assistance, especially the faculty members, for any joint research that can be done. In these years, however, he has been left with much disappointment. After having spoken to more than five hundred faculty members and students, barely four of them are in touch with him. He has also helped a couple of students get placed with organizations from this network, but they rarely called him back either to say a 'thank you' or even inform about the interview call that they had received.

Ravi says that his enthusiasm to meet people and his willingness to help them will never diminish. He echoes the words of Harvey Mackay, who says, 'My golden rule of networking is simple: Don't keep score.'

The concept of networking is not new. We have been networking with people since the beginning of mankind. We do this because human beings are social and we love dealing with people we know. The more familiar we are with people, the easier it becomes for us to connect, convince or persuade. If you know people, things become faster and easier. It may also save you some money. Your networking skills could be giving you some 'extra' discounts at the grocery store, which no customer has a privilege of.

This skill of networking however requires some degree of consistency and perseverance for its success. Networking in itself does not work unless you want to make it work. It will not yield you any result unless you have invested in your network. You may not even want help from your network, but many feel gratified connecting with people. When a seed is sown, it takes months, sometime years for it to bear fruits and flowers and quite so for networking. The important aspect, however, in networking is 'engagement', which means how effectively you keep your network engaged.

What you are trying to do is build a mutually beneficial relation, and this is what networking is.

In earlier days, we used to separate business and personal relationships. With time, people started moving away from their own homes, and this line distinguishing the two thinned. Business and personal relations have become more of a mishmash and there is little line that differentiates the two.

So if you are the introvert kind, do not worry, you have been networking. You need to make a formal start. If you have already been networking, this chapter will help you further your thought process.

Networking as a concept was in a different form altogether even before the rise of the social networking systems and the Internet. Bengali 'addas', for example, were an intellectual exchange among members. Although popular among the middle class, notable film director Satyajit Ray traces it back to Greece in one of his movies.[1]

---

[1] https://en.wikipedia.org/wiki/Adda_(South_Asian) (accessed on 11 May 2019).

Indian coffee houses set up in the colonial period, for example, are a classic example where intellectuals would come together to debate on various issues and thereby network with others. The Bloomsbury Group, for example, was a group of writers, intellectuals, philosophers and artists of British origin.[2] The purpose of all these groups was probably to network for the purpose of a mutually beneficial relationship. All this networking however belonged to a closer group of people, generally not dispersed geographically; however, with the influx of the internet, you now have the provision to connect with people across the globe, though you may not have met even once. Even in such an era, we still value and treasure our networking with people whom we meet face-to-face.

RULES OF NETWORKING

Effective networking isn't a result of luck—it requires hard work and persistence.

—Lewis Howes

Rule number 1: What is there for someone else to connect with you? However even before you try to embark to an answer for this question, it is important to remember that returns may not be measured only in terms of tangible achievements. Liking a post someone has written or sharing their posts with people whom you know are also examples of returns. Tagging someone for a suitable job opportunity, even if he may not be actively seeking a job, recommending someone for a job or even a restaurant is also consideration in some form. It is therefore important to find out what you can give in networking. Therefore, if you have sent a connection request to someone whom you felt the need to connect with, and they did not accept it, just move on.

A lady based out of UK had posted a query on a research networking site about a help required with her doctoral work. She was looking for respondents in the area of project management who could help her with their inputs. Although Rajiv never knew her, he volunteered

---

[2] https://en.wikipedia.org/wiki/Bloomsbury_Group (accessed on 11 May 2019).

to do so and connected with her. He also shared it with couple of his colleagues who could respond back to her.

Rule number 2: It could also happen that there is a person who is sitting idle in your network for couple of years. Suddenly you remember that this guy could be of help. Just because you have a network does not mean that there will be continuous interaction. You could request help from them years later or may be immediately. Therefore, wait patiently either to seek help or to help out people. Just be in touch.

Spandan had a batchmate who was known for his pranks in the class. He was always a last bencher, but they interacted during their MBA. 15 years later, Spandan wrote a book and was looking for someone who could write a foreword for the book. The editor did not give him much time, and he was in a rush. After browsing through a couple of his contacts on LinkedIn, Spandan knew he could rely on this guy. In these 15 years, he had become the head of an organization, leading a well-known networking site. Spandan called him to check if he could do this, and he immediately agreed.

Rule number 3: The right start is work half done. If you are confused on how to make a start, focus on what you can offer. Everyone has something to offer.

Even if you have nothing to offer to the other person, there is nothing wrong in asking, 'How may I help you? Do let me know if I could assist you with anything.'

This in itself is a great start for any person with whom you would want to network with. Similarly, this holds true when I get unsolicited requests. I pose the same question to them. If you are meeting a person face-to-face, the best way is to make the conversations interesting. Refer to the chapter on small talks in this book.

A colleague of Rima left the organization barely a year after she had joined. She did not report to Rima. This was about 10 years back.

They were connected on a social platform, though they did not talk or interact. However, couple of days back she reconnected with Rima, asking for some help. She was applying for a Canadian PR and she needed an experience letter from her past organization. Both her managers whom she reported to had left. She called Rima, however was 'unsure' if she could help her. Rima got her work done finally.

Rule number 4: For any networking to work, ask yourself this question, *what do I tell them about me*? This is about the brand that you are trying to build for yourself. You are telling the audience or your target group that you could be of help in a certain area of your expertise. However, ensure that you do not overdo it or underdo it. Do you want yourself to be projected as a philanthropist, a banker or a golfer? If you wear multiple hats, it is probably better that you project an image that is right for the target audience. Remember that it is your personal brand. You are projecting a picture of yourself and personifying it.

Rule number 5: You do not need to spend extra time to network. You are networking every hour. Meeting your grocery store owner, driver, maid, friends and colleagues is all about networking. Everything that you talk to me about is some form of networking that you are doing. When someone calls you while you are not at home, and you call back, is networking or keeping your neighbour's son for some time at your home is also networking.

Shashi was invited to speak at a conference in Mumbai. Shashi was in Pune for some work and the organizers arranged for her pickup to Mumbai. On the way Shashi started conversing with the driver. Shashi generally does it for two reasons. First he gets to know a lot about people and it helps him be closer to reality. Second in such long journeys (about 3 hours), the person on the wheels is fatigued a lot. Talking to them reduces their fatigue to a great extent. So the driver started talking and asking about Shashi's journey. After sometime he asked for some suggestions about his son and about the opportunities in the corporate world. Before leaving, Shashi gave his visiting card and asked him to contact him in case he needs any help.

In another case Shashi was standing in the security check of the airport. The person checking Shashi saw his official badge and started talking about his son and if there were any suitable opportunities in his organization. Shashi shared his contact details and said he would inform him when a vacancy is announced in the organization.

Rule number 6: Building relationships with people much before you require them is networking. You may or may not benefit from the relationship immediately, but still you wish to share and help with your knowledge. So what is in it for you? If your work gets done easily because of someone you know or you get help when you need from your contacts and the work gets done faster and cheaper, it is networking.

I do not consider it networking when people send me an invite or connect with me and in the first instance start asking me for a job or try selling me something. I also do not consider it networking when they want to use my influence to get things done which are incorrect or beyond the rule books.

Couple of fresh MBA graduates had joined an organization and after the training they were getting posted at a location where their offices were present. One of the candidates was from the institute where the head of the training department had graduated. The trainee found out a batchmate of his and made him call to secure a favourable posting location. The training head flatly refused. This is not networking.

Rule number 7: People keep sending invites to network without actually knowing what to do with them. There are many people who write, 'connected with 10,000+ people'. But do those connections really mean anything? Ask yourself this question, 'can we derive mutual values and benefits, and can I be of some help to this guy?' The second question that you must ask is, 'do I feel really positive and energetic to meet this person and is it worthwhile *(I do not mean tangible)* maintaining a relationship with him?'

John got in touch with the CEO of a company for permission to reproduce a blog he had written. John exchanged a couple of mails and finally the CEO permitted to use his blog post. After receiving the permission, John sent him an invite on a social networking site to connect. He declined it with a note, 'I connect only with people whom I have personally worked with.'

While this may seem a little harsh and John did not see this coming, John appreciated his decision. There was no need to connect in future. The CEO was a technology geek and John was not from his area of expertise.

Rule number 8: If you want to see yourself to be a successful networker, the only rule is to *communicate, communicate* and *communicate.* The first is a warm up conversation, the second is to continue the conversation and maintain the relationship and the third is to help the person or seek his help. While you are baking a cake, the first thing to do is to pre-heat an oven to keep it ready. This is to ensure that the movement to the later stages go on smoothly. This is warming up. You may introduce yourself, thank a person in case he has sent you an invite or made a follow up call if you have met the person. The second stage is when the initial teething trouble is gone. You now know the person. You are now starting to bake your cake. However, the final product is still not ready. You engage the person in further conversations, meet him once or twice a year or more if required, talk about similar interests and discuss things that can be done together. You can also subordinate or help the person with some of his work or even offer to share your time. This is the time to bond. The third is to communicate to seek or provide help. This is when the baked cake is ready. You can provide your support or seek help, such as introducing someone or asking for a suitable opportunity or making the next career move or selling a product or seeking referral. Your communication should be heart appealing for the person receiving it, using a channel that works for both of you. For example, you cannot meet up, but you can talk. Therefore, choose to talk or use a mail.

PLACES TO NETWORK

The currency of real networking is not greed but generosity.

—Keith Ferrazzi

As explained earlier, there is no specific place to network. The easiest way to start is to walk into your office and smile at a person you do not know. Once you have done that, the next step is to talk to the person when you meet the next time. You can just start by saying, 'Sorry we have not been introduced. I am....'

Find out common ways to keep the conversation interesting. Focus on knowing the person in the first meeting. You should do this with people you do not know or with whom you have lost touch with. Pick up the phone and start calling them up. You can make a list of people to do so. The easiest way to start off a telephonic conversation in case you have left is to start with where you had left. For example, 'Do you remember the last time we met, we had this issue of settling our foreign office accounts.' Remind the other person about a pleasurable or not so pleasurable incident which had a happy ending. For example, a meeting which started off with a bitter fight went on to smoothen the relation. Like, 'We started off with the bitter fight and thankfully we settled it down quickly.'

One of my suggestions is to separate personal and professional relationships. Although both are networks and both of them can serve a common purpose, however it is necessary that you treat them separately.

Lakshman did a lot of social work. He used to spend a lot of his time after office doing this. After couple of months, his colleagues came to know about it and spread a rumour that he is doing this during office hours. He got frustrated more about this after his managers hinted at this indirectly. Earlier he used to post all these activities on social media, but later he stopped posting them. He also deactivated his social networking account and befriended all of his office colleagues from another social networking site. He stopped accepting connection invites from anyone who worked with him in his organization.

The first place to network is your current organization and one of the key ways to network is going beyond office hours, finding something of a common interest, such as playing pool or football, and getting along. Our common tendency is to hang around with people we know at office for years. Avoid it if you want to do a good job of networking.

Cut across departments and lines of work. Other places where you can conveniently network are your customers, clients, consultants, external agencies you deal with, conferences you attend, alumni network, travelling in planes or railways, or may be at a trade show.

CONVERSATIONS IN NETWORKING

Conversations are the heart of networking and building relationships. We are communicating at three stages: first, when we meet for the first time; second, when we take the relationship ahead and maintain them and third, when we seek help or give help. Remember that one and three may coincide in some situations. However, it is better that we follow them stage wise.

When you start initiating a conversation, try and find out more about the person. A simple introduction like, 'Hi, I am…We have not met' could take you on for quite some time. Find out more about the person and make a mental note of it. These are the cues which will help you in the next conversation. If the person is talking about a 'Chinese client' who does not understand English well, the next conversation should have some discussions on those topics. People will remember and like you when you share similar things with them and they will appreciate you when you remember them. It builds rapport and they want to listen to you or continue them further. The person standing and listening to you is also judging you. So if are meeting a CEO, talk like a CEO. Ask questions that matter to him the most, like, 'What are the three things that keep you worried about your people?' Questions like these increase your confidence to talk to others, it also makes a conversation memorable.

The best way to start off is by asking neutral questions and finding a common ground. Ask questions about their organization, job and people. If you are networking with people from the same industry, things are relatively easy, like 'What is happening with AI in your organization?' The other easier ways are to ask open-ended questions. Questions such as, 'Since when have you been working for this company?' vis-a-vis 'How has your experience been so far working with this company?' Both these questions though open-ended, allow the person to talk more than what he would have. Listen to what is being said and ask relevant questions. Do not over bother a person by asking too many questions like an interrogation. Talk more about the other person and ensure that you initiate a conversation. If a conversation is not going anywhere, transition to another topic. Appreciating accomplishments and attire is always memorable and a good way to keep a conversation interesting. You can also ask the person if he/she is on LinkedIn or Facebook and check if they would be interested in receiving your connection request. Especially on social networking sites, when you send an invite to a person you know, send a personalized note such as 'It was wonderful meeting you in Mumbai. I would be interested in connecting with you. Please get in touch with me for anything at…(share your contact details).' If you do not know a person, and you are sending an invite, write, 'I am Praveena Mukherjee from Trident Corporation. I take care of sales and marketing for the northern region. I would be interested in connecting with you. Do let me know if I could help you with anything (share your contact details).'

The second stage of networking is when you are being in touch. You can call up the person, email him or meet the person. For example, if you know someone who has written an article and you liked it, you may use this to follow up with the person. Another easy technique is to receive the feed of birthdays on LinkedIn, and spend a minute or two calling the person to wish him. If you feel that there has been a significant gap since the last time you spoke, start with the conversation you had left at or remind him about how both of you met, how memorable it was or something that you shared in common. If you are writing an email, introduce yourself briefly to remind the person with a line, 'Hope you are okay. We had met in the trade conference at Kolkata.' You can keep the conversation going. However, since you know the person already, it is best at this stage not to overshare about yourself.

The third stage of networking is asking for help. Now that you know the person, you can directly approach the person. A query like, 'I am looking for a marketing person who has worked in pharma.

Do you know someone who can help?' or something like, 'I am looking at connecting with Dr Rajeev and he is connected with you. Can you please introduce me?' When you are asking, be specific. Do not dilly-dally. If you cannot help, say so or direct to someone else. Asking someone, 'I am looking for an opening in your company' vis-à-vis, 'I am looking for an opening as a test engineer in your company' is much more specific. If you are trying to sell using your network, specify what you do and what problems you can solve using your solution.

The last of all is to give a gracious exit to the person. If you ask someone, 'Would you know someone who has worked in the pharma industry? We are looking for help in building our distributors in the western region?' The person could say a 'yes' or a 'no'. In both the cases, be gracious and thank him.

PLANNING YOUR NETWORK

> Networking is an investment in your business. It takes time and when done correctly can yield great results for years to come.
>
> —Diane Helbig

Three most common questions that come up in the planning phase of your networking are: How many, whom and why? The first is how many people should be there in my network, the second is whom should I connect with and third is why should I connect with only a set of people from a bigger universe of people. While these questions seem to nag everyone who is networking, they are not too difficult to be answered.

Answering the first question, you may have as little as 100 or as many as infinite number of people in your network. But what matters is the value that you can give them. If you are taking your personal network into consideration and people you generally meet in person and are closer geographically, it will be difficult for you to manage more than 200 to 250 people (you may have your own estimate on this). But more does not mean merrier because you may not be able to give considerable time to each one of them. Therefore, consider the time and efforts that you will have in managing all these people. Let us now go to a virtual network. You may have as many as you want. But will you be sending them a message even once a year. Probably not. You may not even recollect after sometime whether a person is in your network.

Like a person asked Rahul, 'I saw this person in your network. How do you know this guy?' Rahul was clueless. He didn't even know the person even though he was in his network.

The second question is whom should I connect with. Make a laundry list of people whom you already know and club them according to various groups. First are alumni (school, college and university or even a professional program), second are your colleagues, third are your customer and clients, and last are the others on the basis of some common interest, such as cricket, hockey, art, painting and music. Now while you may find plenty of reasons to connect with many people around these key areas, like your graduate school could be having 600 people, you may not be able to connect with all. To further shortlist them down, ask these three questions. First, what is that I can offer? Second, how is the person? Is the person approachable, rude, arrogant and unwilling to respond or great, wonderful and helpful? Do you feel great meeting this person? The third question that you must ask is the relevance as of today. Relevance means does this person fit into the goal or objective for which you are connecting? If the person is irrelevant, it does not mean that you would not connect. For example, your best friend at university is doing something which is not your area of interest. He is not irrelevant. He can still be your network. Ensure however that you have more people who are relevant for the purpose why you are networking.

While connecting you may reach out to people because of two reasons. The first may be with a purpose and the second may be without any purpose. While the first is more strategic like finding the right contact point or a person for a suitable opening, the later may be more open, where you connect because of a similar interest or it may be purely an accidental meeting with a person. While you may encounter both these situations at different points of time, you must have some goal. Ensure that your goal is not too stringent or rigid, but flexible enough.

Kriti had been to an academic conference to promote her earlier book and connect with people, however could not achieve much at the end of the conference. She met a couple of people and a few professors who seem to be very busy running the show rather than listening to Kriti. However, Kriti still connected with people around her and met one person who was willing to talk. After a couple of years, Kriti is still in touch with that person and every year they meet up, although they do not have much to share, they gel well.

Maybe your goal is to hire a person in a niche technology and you want to use your network to find one.

Venkat is a part of his college HR group. It is a group of HR professionals who passed out of the same institute. One of them asked a generic query about the 'work from home policy' and broad guidelines surrounding it. She was formulating a policy for her organization. Venkat offered her help and gave the guidelines of how the policy works for his organization.

Your goals could be finding out about funding for a charitable cause, finding volunteers, taking an advice from people about your next career move, finding out what is the working style of a particular organization that you are joining, hiring new people and asking for a reference.

Revisiting and removing people from your network should be an activity. You may choose to revisit once a year or once in five years or when your network is turning to be unmanageable. The decision rests with you. I was earlier in banking and now I am into information technology. Although I have some good friends in the banking industry, I have phased out most of them from my earlier network. While these were some of the calls that I had to take, I did this because of my personal reasons of not being able to give them time/value and my current area of expertise does not need me to connect with banking professionals and it is very unlikely that I would ever step into banking again.

You need to remove some of the people from your connections and these are either the 'fair weather friends' or the people 'who are a cause of headache'. You will find a plenty of people in either category. I would however suggest not to do things that are unprofessional or support them for an act which is immoral. Just 'stay away' and say 'no'.

Summing it all up: it is left to you to decide who you would like to network with, to remove and keep. Ask yourself this question, 'How many of them (from your contacts) would return your phone call and offer you a help if you would have lost your job?' Or replace this with a more suitable yet tough question to yourself.

MAINTAINING AND TRACKING NETWORK

> Networking is not about just connecting people. It's about connecting people with people, people with ideas, and people with opportunities.

> —Michele Jennae

After you have built your network, you need to duly follow up with them. Following up is taking the relationship ahead. While it may be purely business oriented, you may just want to follow up to be on their minds. Keep tapping them. You may like, share their article, send them a mail and wish them on their birthdays or anything that you can think of. Try and meet your network when you need them as well as when you do not need them. The best way is to meet up for lunch or a cup of coffee. If you chance to visit their city, ensure that you meet couple of them during the visit. At office, never go for lunch or coffee alone or with the same set of people you know. When someone asks you to come out for a coffee during intervals, never refuse, even if you do not want to have a cup. Just accompany them.

During many of these conversations, you get sales pitch from your networks. While there is nothing wrong in saying 'no' in a pleasant way, it is better to direct them to someone who can handle it better. Saying, 'Thank you for sending out this request. Can I please request you to get in touch with Mr Roger? He currently handles this department.' Or you can say, 'I am sorry but I do not know the point of contact.'

For example, a contact of Leena wrote a note to her to sell services for her organization. However, being the wrong contact point, Leena directed her to HR.

If you have sent an invite to some person to join your network and the person is not responding to your messages or you feel that there is something 'cold' about it or things are not clicking, it is time to say 'good bye'. Do not latch on to them/stalk them.

Sameer was doing a consulting assignment. He started his work and after sometime his client refused to pick up his calls. He tried his best to reach out to them, but failed. After couple of tries he realized that probably they were unwilling. He kept quiet. To carry forward the relationship, he used to send them birthday messages to which they reciprocated. Sameer realized that there was something that went wrong, which he did not have any clue about. However, the client was open to maintaining the relationship.

You must know when to come out and when to keep moving ahead. Sometimes there is a sense of desperation to connect to a person for a job or some help. In such a hurry we often tap on the topic too soon. While this might be okay for some, it may not be for others. Be wary about these situations. Avoid rushing or tapping your network unless you know them very well or at least you have given them a chance. If you really need to tap your contacts immediately, then it is a high-risk bet.

When someone from your network connects with you for some help which you may or may not be able to give, state that explicitly. Do not keep the person hanging around. Keep the commitments that you have made. If you cannot, either decline politely or redirect them to someone could possibly them help out.

Some of other ways to maintain and grow are to join online groups, groups of people with similar hobbies or interests, meeting people personally, writing a post or having a blog, joining community service, sharing articles, job postings to your networks, liking a post or commenting on them or sending a thank you note. There are a plenty of ways. When you write or speak in a conference, invite them to come down. Check if they would be interested to participate. If you are unable to accept any invitation for talking in a seminar, direct it to someone in your network.

When I want a fast and quick response from my network, I always prefer my alumni. They are the easiest to connect with. They are the ones who are most unlikely to refuse any of my requests. In fact, very few have refused. They find out ways in getting the things done. Similarly, when I have an opportunity, they are the first ones that come to my mind. When people ask me for references, I first think about my alumni base. Only when no one fits into the requirements, I refer them to others.

Similarly, you must keep in touch with your clients and alumni. Keep interacting with them and find out ways you can add value to the group or them individually.

Sameer had a friend from college who worked as an anchor for a national sports channel. After he joined the channel, almost the entire batch started watching the particular channel. After the match they had discussions on what went wrong, what he said and had some serious fun about it. They also recommended the channel to other people.

If you are doing something different, people are very likely to appreciate you. If you are taking up some cause, use it as an opportunity to network with people.

While you are busy growing your network keep away from toxic people. These people drain you in every possible way and there is no way you get to benefit from them. They also treat relationships as a transaction and therefore the best way to manage them is to 'keep away' from them. An arm's length distance is not okay. Stay miles away.

CONCLUSION

You just cannot do away with networking. Treat interactions as investments and not withdrawals. The more you invest, the more you can withdraw. If you avoid meeting people, then there must be a reason to do so. If you are doing that occasionally, it is okay. But avoid being on the couch every time and expect things to happen. Prepare the grounds of networking well before you require them. One of the common things that the non-networking kinds tell me is their fear of talking to people. They get tight-lipped when they start talking. They do not know what to talk about. Unless you make the first move, no one is really bothered. A classified was published which said, 'Dear beautiful lady, I met you for the first time at the library. However, I did not get the courage of talking to you. Can you please call me at the numbers given below?' Unfortunately, no call came for this gentleman. If you can give more value than what you take, you are doing it the best. If you are worried about what you can give, introspect and there will be qualities and traits that others would envy you for.

4 Meaningful Conversations: Frameworks of Long-Lasting Business

Let us make a special effort to stop communicating with each other, so we can have some conversation.

—Mark Twain

'People do not listen with the intent to understand; they listen with the intent to reply', is one of the famous quotes by renowned communication specialist Stephen R. Covey. In essence, this implies that a conversation becomes powerful when the focus is on learning instead of educating, that is, when you become the student rather than the teacher.

This approach could actually be a mind-blowing game changer for you at work. In this chapter, we will read what transforms a superficial interaction into a meaningful conversation for a long-lasting business.

Godfrey Hardy, professor of mathematics at Cambridge was visiting his friend, Srinivas Ramanujan who was unwell. After the day's work, Professor Hardy took a taxi to Ramanujan's place. After reaching his house and exchange of pleasantries, Professor Hardy mentioned to Ramanujan that he came in a taxi.

Ramanujan: So Prof, what was the taxi number in which you had come?

Prof Hardy: Oh…A very boring number indeed. It was 1729.

Ramanujan: Prof, that was not at all boring. In fact, a very interesting number…It is the smallest number that could be expressed by the sum of two cubes in two different ways.

This conversation is not only famous among mathematicians, but is referred to as the 'Hardy–Ramanujan number' or the 'taxicab' number. This fact was however not discovered by Ramanujan himself, but a French mathematician Bernard Frénicle de Bessy. Conversations could be a lot more interesting, fun and a wonderful experience for all. They could be engaging and inspiring, leaving the other person feeling perfectly understood. Ramanujan made a dull conversation extremely interesting with his ability to present a fact discovered long ago.

THE FLIGHT FROM CONVERSATION

Conversation is a meeting of minds with different memories and habits. When minds meet, they don't just exchange facts: they transform them, reshape them, draw different implications from them, and engage in new trains of thought. Conversation doesn't just reshuffle the cards: it creates new cards.

—Theodore Zeldin

In the silence of connection, comfort has given birth to technologically-driven people who want to be in touch with lot of people, however carefully kept at bay. Good conversations have become rare. Millennials are texting more and talking less.[1] JPMorgan Chase, one of the largest banking institutions in the USA, therefore decided to eliminate voicemail, saving US$3 million annually. Millennials employed texts, emails and social media to reach out to people rather than conversing.

---

[1] Neil Howe, 'Why Millennials Are Texting More and Talking Less,' *Forbes*, 15 July 2015, https://www.forbes.com/sites/neilhowe/2015/07/15/why-millennials-are-texting-more-and-talking-less/#3e3ccbb15975 (accessed on 26 May 2019).

Conversations could be defined as the 'oral exchange of sentiments, observations and opinions'. I prefer to define conversations as the 'art' of communicating and exchanging ideas, feelings and thoughts to another person or a group of persons. They have the ability to connect you with people, make or break a relationship, put your reputation at stake or help to create an everlasting impression. Conversations have an innate power: A power to listen to diverse ideas and thoughts of others, thereby enriching oneself.

They can be set up in formal environments, for example, when you discuss business, promotions or negotiate with your vendors, and informal ones, for example, when you go out for a cup of coffee or a soccer match with your manager. Also categorized into 'short talk' and 'long talk' depending on the duration of the conversation, people refer to the longer and formal ones as conversations. As a professional, both have their own significance.

OUTCOME-BASED CONVERSATIONS

While most professional conversations are targeted to achieve an outcome, they often become difficult when participants do not think alike or disagree with each other. This is quite normal. However, the way the conversation is shaped further is what matters, which in many cases turns into a superimposition of ideas on the other person.

Remember, conversations are an exchange of ideas, NOT a superimposition on others. It is not yelling at others, 'I am right and you are wrong.' It is about listening to ideas of others and encouraging people to speak their minds to create a pool of ideas that will realize a higher value or goal. For example, the sales figures have been falling and you are having a conversation with your sales team essentially to understand what can be done to improve. Conversations are critical in decision-making. Decisions taken with cognizance of larger group of people have a better buy-in than taken in smaller groups. With diverse ideas and backgrounds, people will differ. People who converse are convinced that he/she is putting forward the right set of arguments, unless challenged. However, one should always remember that the purpose of a professional conversation is to achieve a common ground—a successful outcome, which is based on how we handle the conversation. Look at the conversation between Bill Gates and Steve Case and why it became difficult as a result of a misunderstanding of the words spoken vis-a-vis the meaning.

Steve Case, CEO of AOL, met Bill Gates in May of 1993. AOL was moderately successful with its MSN services, while Bill Gates was the third-largest service provider online. The meeting was about possible opportunities for the two companies to collaborate. Infamously, Gates told Case, 'I can buy 20 per cent of you or I can buy all of you. Or I can go into this business myself and bury you.' Case replied, 'My Company is not for sale.'[2]

Microsoft asserted that Gates was 'thinking out loud'. But AOL executives took Gate's words as a threat to their company.[3]

There must be an outcome of a conversation. A conversation may be either to discuss ideas or simply talk about the issues at the organization, exchange information pertaining to decision-making or the productivity issues of a unit or department. It could be a discussion on the list of promotions in the next cycle. However, there must be an outcome of all conversations.

Conversation is Like Riding a Bicycle

A conversation is a dialogue, not a monologue. That's why there are so few good conversations: due to scarcity, two intelligent talkers seldom meet.

—Truman Capote

A question commonly asked is, 'What constitutes a great conversation?' While the answers would differ depending on the perspective you get to hear, but there are certain aspects which you must get right.

---

[2] Laura Lambert, Chris Woodford, Hilary Poole and Christos J. P. Moschovitis, (Ed) *The Internet: A Historical Encyclopedia Biographies,* (Santa Barbara, CA: ABC CLIO, 2005), 55.

[3] Brian McCullough, *How the Internet Happened: From Netscape to the iPhone* (New York, NY: Liverright Publishing Corporation, 2018).

The first and foremost is ensuring that conversations are balanced. Conversations are like riding a bicycle where you need to keep your balance or else you will fall.

Similarly, falling back heavily to one side of a discussion or argument, that is, on the 'politically correct' side could make it boring, irrelevant and catastrophic to the final outcome. It would leave the participants in an awe and would be more of a 'monologue' than a 'dialogue', which dilutes the purpose to converse.

The new head of a training department decided to make some dramatic transformations to increase the productivity. She doubled the number of training days each quarter. This change did not go well with the trainers. In one of the 'open houses', she started speaking about her future plans for the department, while the trainers asked her some questions on the rationale behind the increased training days. The point of view that the trainers had was that the current workload did not account for other activities apart from training. After one or two questions from the trainers, and the trainers trying hard to reason out with data and facts on why it would be difficult, the head of the training department refused to answer any further questions. There was stoic silence in the room. For the next hour, it was the head who was speaking and no one in the audience had the urge or willingness to ask any further questions.

Balanced conversations mean the proportion of talking that we do vis-a-vis listening, and the balance given to the start, middle and the end of the conversation. A lot of talking done to impress the people sitting for a 'conversation' could backfire. Balanced would mean 'understanding' the right context of a conversation. Sometimes we feel we are on track, however we could be wrong.

In a presentation for a new IT project, the members of a sales team were all enthusiastically trying to make a sales pitch to a client. The sales team spoke for an hour and then finally after a pause....

Client: We really liked your pitch.

Sales team: Thank you. We are the consultants who have done

business with Fortune 500 companies and the average size of our deal is 50 to 100 million dollars.

(After naming some clients in the Fortune 500, the sales person stopped.)

Client: Now this is what worries me. Will you even take any interest in a project as small as ours? Ours is not even 10 per cent the size of the average deals that you do. My worries are that you will not even be able to allocate resources to our small project.

Sales team: (Dumb struck…did not expect that coming)

As people converse, listening and talking about *diverse viewpoints* are important. Diverse viewpoints enrich discussions and present all possibilities to a situation. They give the listener a sense of importance and the group a larger goal or a pool of thoughts on which it can fall back upon. It is then best to leave the participants to understand the best course of action to be taken in such situations. While you listen avoid multi-tasking. That would reflect sincerity on your part.

Business meaningfulness of conversations is important. Subjects unimportant, irrelevant and untimely will withdraw people away from the conversation. For example, talking about budgets for lesser important priorities when the company is trying to cut costs.

Business was going down due to global recession. The young kid who had just joined walked into the office of a senior manager.

Manager: So how is it going on?

Trainee: Going great sir. It is a wonderful place.

Manager: Have you started working on your new project?

Trainee: No sir…Still on the knowledge transfer phase.

Manager: Please take this up quickly. We are working on cutting costs. Your new work will help us save costs on the new projects we undertake.

Trainee: Sir, I was wondering if you could sponsor me for this conference (global conference). This will help me enable in another technology.

Manager: We will not be able to. (And walks away)

We rarely converse with the outcome in mind and that becomes the recipe to a pathetic conversation. Starting a conversation with the end in mind is a good start. 'Outcome-based balanced conversations' achieve results and keep the discussion on track. Discussions in business should either be able to resolve a problem, generate ideas or explore solutions to existing problems. Outcome-based does not mean that we approach a conversation with a pre-fixed mindset. For example, going for a sales review call with an idea to howl or pounce upon the sales team is wrong. The right outcome would be 'to understand the current status and suggest a possible course of action'. If you are going with a fixed mindset, people will either avoid such conversations or agree with whatever you say, just to disagree with you later. For budgeting, sales managers often use words like, 'This is the figure that I am looking at for the next cycle.' This in itself is a detriment to a great conversation as you are limiting yourself within your own boundaries.

KEEP CONVERSATIONS 'FREE-FLOWING'

Conversations that are inhibited, stopped, interrupted or presented with ideas which are pre-mediated or fabricated rarely serve a purpose. They would better be called as an 'eyewash'. When the flow of thought gets curtailed, participants hesitate to open up, thereby impeding the basic purpose of having a conversation. Great conversationalists will first attempt to break this barrier and give all the ideas a fair chance to be heard even if they are controversial or non-mainstream.

HR of a large MNC firm sent out an email to the employees asking them to join an 'open house' with the CEO. The CEO had been appointed recently and had planned his tour to all the India offices, essentially to understand the pulse of the organization. In the Delhi and Kolkata meet, the employees asked the CEO some questions pertaining to the working policy of the organization and raised issues which were bothering them. Although the CEO sidestepped them and appeared ignorant, he knew the other offices would act similarly. He directed the HR to collect questions from the employees before-hand under the pretext of saving time. During the Bangalore visit, the CEO was posed with questions from the HR only about topics that were 'safe' and 'non-political' to talk about. The employees realizing this started walking out of the venue.

> Be brave enough to start a conversation that matters.
>
> —Margaret Wheatley

The following are the challenges in conversations:

- Avoiding it
- Unwillingness to agree to others' ideas
- Balancing between talking and listening
- Keeping it simple (KISS: Keep it simple, silly)
- Irrelevant and close-ended questions

Imagine the next meeting with your client manager. The project is complete and you know that there is no more business that is going to come. The client sets a closure call with your team. You excuse yourself and ask the next in line to attend.

Or a situation when you are neck-deep in work. A reportee comes to you worried and anguished. She wants to talk.

She: Can we talk for some time? This is really urgent.

You: Didn't you see my messenger status, before walking in?

Conversations can be handled in three ways. First is to take it casually or half-heartedly. Phrases such as 'let us see', 'wait and watch' or 'can we do it some other time' are frequently used in such conversations. Second is to take the bull by the horns and give in your best. The third is, of course, to avoid.

Venky used to avoid Anju because of her pestering nature. She would invariably divert or hijack a discussion and would spend quite some time relentlessly discussing about issues which were trivial. Every time that she would be around, Venky would find out a way to run away. Even if they met in the cafeteria, Venky used to walk away from her. If Venky had to communicate or converse with her, the safest way was to hide behind an email or pass the message to someone who would communicate it to Anju.

If you ask me, I would say that the bigger challenge lies in avoiding conversations. In the early years of my corporate career, I avoided conversations. I barely spoke, leaving others confused about a person who excelled in selling. Certain situations were surely tough for me, such as announcing a promotion to a very close friend at the same level or firing a subordinate. I found short talks 'unmanageable'. I never knew where to begin and end. I froze with fear every time I had to do a small talk. The bigger problem however were the mental blocks that would freeze my mind of ideas to death.

While half-hearted attempt is equally bad, it is still better than the former. A little conscious attempt on changing the attitude can help get over this.

Ideas and thoughts of people are unlikely to be similar. And in cases that we find these ideas difficult to agree with, we disagree. We do not listen to different ideas with the similar degree of openness as we would with our own ideas. We mentally overrule ideas that challenge our existing thoughts, processes and beliefs. We attach great importance to what we say and are emotionally connected to it. We are willing to defend or fight off every evil that challenges the process of thought that we nurture. Listening to the opinions of others requires a great deal of sincerity. You do not need to fake sincerity. If you are genuinely interested, you will be sincere and so will be the listening. Being sincere is a great challenge in conversations.

Conversations need a balance between talking and listening, and we have lost that balance. Your idea may not be supreme, and in case you do feel so, please avoid a conversation. Just thrust it down to your people. Avoid wasting your time to converse if you feel your ideas and thoughts are out of this world. Therefore, just as you talk, you 'listen'. If you are unwilling to listen, then people will be unwilling to talk.

Conversations need not be complex. Stick to the KISS approach of conversing. 'Keep it simple, silly.' Conversations which are long-drawn out, and burdened with facts and figures are boring and we inevitably turn them into a complex discussion. Participants will take lesser interest in such conversations. While details are necessary, it does not mean you need to sit on a mountain of data. Presenting the bare essentials is all that is needed in a good conversation. Repetition is another killer of great conversations. Often participants tend to raise similar sounding issues, using different words. These become repetitive and monotonous. It is important to present an idea only once.

Asking irrelevant and close-ended questions are some other conversation killers. Asking questions about things that do not matter or divert the discussion to another topic, hijacking topics by other members and having parallel discussions are time wasters. Conversations in such environment lose focus. Asking close-ended questions like, 'Do you think this would work?' Kill the ideas and the thoughts behind them as the answer to them is obviously a 'yes' or a 'no' and these questions do not require any explanations.

> The real art of conversation is not only to say the right thing at the right place but to leave unsaid the wrong thing at the tempting moment.
>
> —Dorothy Nevil

SETTING THE GROUND

> Conversations will never happen the way you want them to. It is important to stay focused on the purpose with which the conversation was started.

You are the national head of sales. Last year was not great and you have been touring frequently last month across branches trying to understand what went wrong. However, in all the branches, the otherwise jubilant and energetic sales team has been keeping silent. You wonder why? Before the round of talks started, the CEO had sent you a stern message, 'Get over this in the next quarter. All our key figures are down and pressure is building upon me.' Things are not right and these words have been 'ringing' in your head. You also need to understand what went wrong last year.

While you reflect about the sales meets that you had, you can remember only one single thing. You had lost your temper owing to the poor performance of the team. This has been at the back of your mind all through. You also conclude that probably this is the message that has been doing the rounds in the other offices and therefore the team is not willing to open up. You know very well that in case they do not open up, your problem is far away from resolution as the sales team can only talk about the ground realities.

In the next meeting at Delhi, you present a different version of yourself, keeping all your apprehensions aside. You encourage your sales team to open up and present their side of the story. While they bring in a lot of ideas and thoughts, you simply make a note of them, keeping your personal views aside. Things start improving for the other sales meets as well. You get a set of very good ideas that are workable and worth working upon.

Ideas from different people bring a larger thought process and help steer the conversation. However, along with these a baggage comes along that steers us. This baggage includes pre-conceived emotions, values and beliefs. Therefore, the person leading the conversation should first ensure sufficient *openness*. With openness, more thoughts are generated, therefore decision-making becomes simpler. Second with diverse ideas, the problem can be looked at from multiple perspectives. Encouraging people to present diverse thoughts and ideas which may not be politically right or may not be pleasing to the ears. Third as a result of the above two, more facts arise, which ultimately weed out the irrelevant facts and half-truths, thereby making the outcomes tangible.

Just as people participating in a conversation come with pre-conceived ideas and notions, so do you. Keep an open mind. Be willing to listen to new things, ideas and thoughts. If you have a bias towards an idea, you will be quick to turndown other ideas and thoughts. Therefore, come to a conversation with an open mind. Steer yourself clear of what you already know. Therefore, start with 'me' rather than 'them'. Knowingly or unknowingly in organizations we also have our own set of mistakes and are a part of the bigger problems. Therefore, setting a part of the onus on 'me' first makes sense than correcting the 'us'.

Keep a simultaneous check on your emotions. Will you tell your manager that his last marketing idea just 'bombed' because he took some irrational decisions? Probably not. Even if you do, you will be sober and toned down in your comments. Even if you are not toned down, the other person may out rightly reject your feelings and emotions or take it in a way that harms the future course of the conversation.

While having a business discussion, it is suggested that keep your feelings out of the window and stick to the agenda. Dealing with feelings is difficult and perhaps the biggest challenge in any conversation.

'Stay focused' during a conversation. Others might try to hijack you or your own ideas might hijack, but stay focused on the discussion that is happening.

You will encounter numerous challenges of counteracting ideas and emotions, but it is important to stay focused on the purpose with which the conversation was started. Therefore, be clear of what you want. In the business context, staying focused would also mean coming with a clear agenda. If you have an agenda, state it right in the beginning.

Some conversations will never yield results no matter how much you try. Steer yourself away from such conversations. They become a waste of time. For example, your subordinate has been creating challenges for you and his other colleagues. You have mentored him, coached him, scorned him and rebuked him, but he refuses to change. Finally, you have decided to move him out of your team. Any discussion at this point of time will rarely be fruitful. Conversations which will yield little value are the ones which are best avoided. Therefore, ensure that you are entering the right conversations and spending quality time listening to the ideas of others to move to a higher platform from where you initially started.

A new e-learning material has been purchased by an organization and the senior management wants employees to access it and at least learn one course in the next month.

Janak: Ram, can you please ensure that the employees log in to the new e-learning material and complete one course in the next one month. The senior managers will draw a report after a month.

Ram: Sir, I can try.

Janak: Ram, this is very pessimistic of you. Why would you want to try? It is absolutely doable. Just push the employees.

Ram: Ok.

Ram later in the evening asks his friend over a cup of coffee, 'Do you think the employees will complete? Half of them are travelling and we have many people who are on leave and a new batch of trainees have joined the office. Who will be responsible for them?'

Friend: Why didn't you tell them?

Ram: What is the use? Someone who does not want to listen, cannot be spoken to....

> Conversation isn't about proving a point; true conversation is about going on a journey with the people you are speaking with.
>
> —Ricky Maye

The following are the basic premises of conversations

- No one is right or wrong
- Stop the arguments and the blame game

- Listening and empathizing is a basic premise
- Encircle a conversation with an environment of 'trust'

The sales cycle was starting and Manohar, the branch head, had been instructed to hand over a new sales kit to the team. Manohar forgot about it, and just a day before their sales cycle suddenly remembered about the brochure. He had assigned the work to Rajesh, his direct reportee. Realizing the mistake, he called up Rajesh and asked him about the status.

Manohar: Where is the sales kit I had asked you to prepare?

Rajesh: I had kept a sample copy on your table long back. I had also sent you an email and also asked the office secretary to inform you about it.

Manohar: Wasn't it your responsibility to come and tell me. Am I unreachable on my cell phone? What was your great idea behind not calling me?

Rajesh: I had tried reaching you as well, but could not get through.

Manohar: (Checking for the kit on his table, he found it. He flipped through a couple of pages)

Manohar: What have you sent across? This is absolute nonsense. I told you very clearly to put the latest data set and the right labels. You have not done it. Some of the errors which I had asked you to correct are not done. The tables have not been aligned.

Rajesh: Manohar, I told you very clearly that I was unwilling to do this. I did not have much time at hand. All my guys were busy in year-end closing and we took the extra burden on us. And unless you are there to guide us on what you exactly want, how will we do it? There were absolutely no guidelines from you.

Manohar: I had given you a summary of what was needed to be done. We had a short discussion.

Rajesh: Yes, I have done all of them. The labelling is absolutely correct. Although the alignment of the figures is incorrect, it is not looking odd. Also before sending it for final print, I had sent you a final copy over email. You did not respond to that as well. I have put all the data in the kit that you wanted.

Manohar: This is no excuse. When a task has been given to you and you have willingly accepted it, you should take end-to-end responsibility of closing it.

Rajesh: There is no point of discussing this Manohar. If you cannot give us time about a work that you want to get done, I cannot do anything about it (hangs up the phone).

In the above conversation, *no one is right or wrong*. Both have their own points of view. The problem is that the argument can go on further and there is no end to superimposing the views on one another. We all present our views with the information that we have at hand, interpret them and come to a conclusion. All of these phases would be different for every person and therefore viewpoints would be different. In our case, if you hear the arguments or interpretations of Manohar and Rajesh individually, you will get to hear two different cases completely. Conversations typically tend to discuss these inter-pretations that we have. These interpretations are also biased towards we wanted or a reflection of our interest. *This is the first lesson for a meaningful conversation; no one is right or wrong.*

If Rajesh and Manohar would have continued their discussions further, there would have never been an end to it. There is no end to how much we can argue. Rajesh would not have agreed with Manohar and vice-versa. Arguments start turning bitter and when you nurture them for long, they turn ugly and uglier. Arguments are never a feasible solution to a problem. The problem is both the parties think the problem lies with the other. If you ever get to hear both of them, individually, both of them will convince you that the other party is at wrong. Sticking to our own stand, or doggedness in general, leads to arguments. Arguments would never arise if we tell ourselves, 'Look the problem lies with me, and I am unwilling to admit.' *This is the second lesson to a meaningful conversation: stop the arguments and the blame game.*

Step into the ideas of the other person standing in front of you, try to understand where he drives his point from and what he ultimately wants from a discussion. It is important to be inquisitive and enquire about what you do not know but the other person does. These points of view will help you keep an overall balance to the overall conversation, and help create a win-win situation. Although we may feel that we know it all, especially about others and more so about 'ourselves', we in fact do not. Our responses are shaped by the environment that drives us, our instincts and our feelings, beliefs and emotions. Things happen fast and even before we have been successful in comprehending we start reacting. *Therefore, listening and empathizing is a basic premise for a great conversation.* This however is not easy. Looking at the viewpoint of others is difficult because their stories are different and the points of view as well. Had Rajesh and Manohar stepped into the shoes of each other, they probably would have at least realized that there were two sides to the coin and neither of them was factually incorrect. The need therefore to argue would have been reduced. If they had not taken a step towards the path of resurrection, the result of this conversation would have been a spoilt relationship.

Encircle a conversation with an environment of 'trust'. Conversations must and should have a safety net. Unless you make the other person confident that the trust remains in the conversations, ideas will not pour into the pool of thoughts. In the above conversation, both of them were busy accusing one another and there was very little done to build trust. Had one of them taken the step aside to build trust, either by the means of acknowledgement or tried to find the best possible path or believed that they cared about each other, it would not have left a bitter feeling. One of the prime reasons why conversations backfire is because of the element of 'trust' missing in it. People tend to misinterpret and even the best of the intentions can turn into an issue. Building a common ground in such environment is essential to build a quotient of trust. *Mutual trust therefore remains a premise for a great conversation.*

Good conversation is as stimulating as black coffee, and just as hard to sleep after.

—Anne Morrow Lindbergh

PUTTING THINGS INTO ACTION

Now that you have a pool of ideas on which great conversations are built, it is time to take a turn into actionizing 'great conversations'. From the beginning of this chapter, I have been focusing on 'outcome-based conversation'. Conversation which does yield any result is a gossip or a chit chat. The outcome to any conversation must be tangible. While you might be out to convince your sales team to perform better or the quality team to look into their performance parameters or ways and means of reducing costs, all of these should lead to suitable action. It is also important to remember that conversations necessarily *do not* mean you are taking the decisions. Sometimes the leadership would decide the course of action, and sometimes you. Organizational-wide changes to the performance appraisal process would be a decision that would rest with the senior management, however promotions in your team could be on you.

It is therefore recommended that you let the people participating know the decision-making process. This can be done in the context setting. You can also use this context setting effectively to lay the ground rules and build 'trust'.

Decision-making can be done in four ways. First is to be sole decision-making authority leaving no scope for others. Second, of course, is to vote. The side with larger votes win. The third style is to take advice from external observers about a particular decision that is going to be taken. The last is to build consensus among people who are conversing. You can use a mix of methods. For example, building a consensus and then voting or in case there is no consensus, asking an external observer to take a decision or referring to a higher authority for a decision.

Each one would have their own set of advantages and disadvantages. For example, people in the organization may not like the first process, however it becomes the only tool when decisions are critical like employee benefits and compensations. Voting is an easier option, and used frequently by law makers and government agencies. While this is an easier process, this becomes difficult to execute when the subject of the discussion is of complex nature. Also people who vote against always tend to block anything happening in the regard. Third is to hire an external observer—used in cases of arbitration, for example, where the decision of the external party is binding on all. Organizations hire consultants to present a neutral view of opinions and take a decision. The last of course is to build consensus. This is the most participative of all approaches, however the most difficult and time consuming. However, the bigger advantage of this method lies in the enthusiastic participation of all.

The next step is to finalize the decision-making process, document the discussion, follow it up and close the open issues in the conversations. A closure note is appreciable.

BIBLIOGRAPHY

1. Inc.com, 'Most People Handle Difficult Situations by Ignoring Them—And the Fallout Isn't Pretty,' *Inc.com*, 22 August 2018, https://www.inc.com/michael-schneider/70-percent-of-employees-avoid-difficult-conversations-their-companies-are-suffering-as-a-result.html (accessed on 26 May 2019).

2. Kerry Patterson, Joseph Grenny, Ron McMillan and Al Switzler, *Crucial Conversations: Tools for Talking When Stakes Are High*, 2nd ed. (New York, NY: McGraw-Hill, 2012).

3. Susan Scott, *Fierce Conversations: Achieving Success at Work and in Life, One Conversation at a Time* (New York, NY: Berkley Books, 2004).

5 The Art of Small Talk

ave you ever peeled an onion? Small talk is like peeling an onion. You reach the core only when you have peeled all the layers off. Peeling the layers is difficult. They bring tears, but the final outcome is enjoyable. The process of peeling could be made more interesting and this is what makes a small talk interesting. Small talk is also an extension of your personality.

The notion about small talk is that it is 'a polite conversation about unimportant things that people make at social occasions.' Let's look at a short talk example and understand it better.

The following is a small talk from the 1994 classic, *The Shawshank Redemption*, where Morgan Freeman as 'Redding' is talking to the Parole board.

Parole Board Interviewer: Please, sit down. Ellis Boyd Redding, your files say you've served 40 years of a life sentence. You feel you've been rehabilitated?

Redding: Rehabilitated? Well, now, let me see. You know, I don't have any idea what that means.

Parole Board Interviewer: Uh, well, it means you're ready to re-join society.

Redding: I know what you think it means, sonny. To me, it's just a made up word, a politician's word, so that young fellas like yourself can wear a suit and a tie and have a job. What do you really wanna know? Am I sorry for what I did?

Parole Board Interviewer: Well, are you?

A small talk can happen multiple times during a day at the workplace—while waiting to meet a client, at the reception, at lunch, inside an elevator and so on. While 'shy' people consider this to be an 'anxiety', many enjoy this. Many choke in their throats at the mere idea of conversing with people, as a result of which they are left out and are named as reserved and distant.

A small talk serves as a bridge between unfamiliarity and conversations. Even if you have known the other person, small talk helps to stabilize an environment before the actual conversations begin. It acts as an appetizer before an entree. It acts as an icebreaker, laying the foundation for a conversation and establishing a connection. It is also suggested not to jump in a conversation without a short talk. It helps shorten the gaps, build warmth and fill in the voids if any. It also helps others feel valued, warm and comfortable.

BIG OPPORTUNITIES KNOCK WITH SMALL TALK

If you are the one who does not know how to make a small talk, there is no need to panic. If you are an introvert or shy, you can still build this most important skill. It requires some effort from you to make certain changes on how you approach people with short talk.

I was searching for an internship during my MBA. I had visited a couple of companies, trying to place my profile. However, without any success.

Later that evening, one of my batchmates told me that there was an alumni meet happening in Bangalore and checked if I would want to visit. I was unwilling, however upon pestering, I agreed.

I reached the venue and was in no mood to talk. I sat near the bar, asked for a coke and started sipping it with some wafers. An alumni walked towards me, asked for a drink and looked at me.

He said: 'I am Samarth, from the 1995 batch.'

Me: (unwillingly) Current batch sir. Hory Sankar.

Samarth: Hory, you do not look fine. I can see a frown on your face. What is the issue?

Me: (unwillingly) Nothing sir. Trying for an internship. Could not get any.

Samarth: (takes out a card) Hory, here it goes. Please call me on Wednesday. I will try and place you in my organization.

Me: (looking at the card and bubbling with joy) thank you, sir. This means a lot to me. I will call you.

Samarth headed a Fortune 500 company. I got the internship and a chance to work under him for three months.

I was foolish. There were many in the alumni meet who could have possibly given me an internship. However, even if that was not the case or my ultimate purpose, I should have made efforts to meet the people, but I did not. Although Samarth started the conversation, ideally I should have. Samarth being a leader of a large organization, was enthusiastic in meeting new people. That day I learnt a big lesson in my life, 'Go out and meet people.'

The first step, therefore, is to *initiate the talk*. You will need to step ahead and talk because unless you do not talk, no one is really bothered about you; therefore, your prerogative is to take the first step.

What do you do next now that you have started? It moves to the next logical step, which is to *continue conversing*. You will have to find out ways to continue, bring in some humour, cheer, bridge gaps and build relationships. Easier said than done. Many people ask or talk about things that are idiotic and kill the interest of others. 'What do you do?' is the perfect question to kill a conversation and that is what we mostly do. Or they rub the wrong side of a person asking them very personal questions. In worse cases, they do not know 'what to talk about' and fall silent half the way through their dinner.

The third step is to *understand if the person is equivocal in his responses*. If they are, then it is time to drop the conversation. In case he shows willingness, it is time to launch the bigger conversation or sign off if need be.

However, small talks do not happen automatically. It is also not about flowing with the conversation. If you can make the other person feel comfortable and at ease, you have done a great job.

HOW DOES SHORT TALK INFLUENCE?

While you are sitting with a stylist, doctor or in a restaurant, don't you like it when they make the experience better with what they talk about? If you do, then surely short talks do have the power to influence. It also gives a positive environment to talk and discuss, thus leaving a positive outcome.

We generally like to do business and meet with people we know, and find ourselves comfortable around them. However, small talks are not only for the people you know in a group but also for the people you do not know. It is putting your focus on your connections and non-acquaintances. Small talks, therefore, help in mutual understanding and building the necessary trust. They also help you build a positive image about yourself, which will help you be remembered amongst all the others present.

If you had a pleasant small talk with a person, you tend to remember it more than the actual conversations.

In today's world, we are moving tremendously fast. Our lives are so busy that we rarely get the time to engage people in conversations. However, people appreciate it when they are listened and spoken to. These are the investments that you are making, which are risk-free. For individuals in business, it must be an inherent part of your skill set. It will not only help you connect with people around but make you more likeable and approachable. You also tend to feel good and rejuvenated at the end of a small talk. An excerpt from the popular book titled, *How to Get a Job on Wall Street*, by Scott Hoover, reads, 'In trying to generate business, the deal pitch is obviously critical. What is not so obvious is that simple, seemingly innocuous conversation with potential clients can be just as important. Companies want to hire people who can think on their feet.'

A small talk, for example, could lead you into a better job or a sales opportunity and also opens up a world of experiences of people which they otherwise would not share.

START A CONVERSATION: NOW

The Tremeloes in their album *The Boat That Rocked* sung, 'Silence is Golden' which reached the top position in the late 1960s. It became a top 100 song in 1967 and sold one million copies globally.

But is silence really golden? The answer is a flat 'NO'. In today's business world, you need to get up and meet people, silence no more remains golden. A stranger no longer remains a stranger the moment you start talking to them. Similarly, someone who is your close friend today was a stranger at some time in your life.

In a meeting, before you are formally introduced to another person by the host or your manager, you can always walk up and say, 'Hi, I am Sankar. It is wonderful meeting you.' This when done with a small smile and eye contact is all that is needed to start off any conversation.

Imagine a situation when you are at a dinner with lot of other people from your organization. You may know some, but ensure that you do not keep searching for them throughout the dinner. Make the efforts to go and meet at least some of the people whom you do not know. I had a manager who used to ensure that for a lunch or a dinner we do not sit with the same people we know. He used to exchange the seats on purpose and ask people to move from a particular table and join other tables.

DO ICEBREAKERS REALLY BREAK THE ICE?

This can be followed by an introductory para—do icebreakers really work? The answer is yes, and we will see in this chapter how they work. Before understanding the icebreaker approach, first you need to identify where the ice is—where does the opportunity lie? What if while waiting for the right opportunity, there may be other opportunities nearby.

Often, we tend to wait for meeting the right person. However, the right or the 'big' person may be busy with his associates or colleagues. He may not be in a position to give you some quality time. It is better that we use the time in meeting others. Therefore, after a quick round of mixing with your acquaintances, ensure you meet the new people in the room as well.

The next step is to start with some classical icebreakers. The objective here is to warm up the conversation. Remember it is your prerogative to drive the conversation. Classical icebreakers can often be boring, such as asking, 'How are you doing?' or 'What do you do?' While these are okay to be used, they do not solicit great responses or invoke involvement. The responses to these queries are generally a word or two. You can alternatively ask, 'What brings you here?', 'How did you get this wonderful idea of starting off on your own?' or 'What is the best thing of being an entrepreneur? Social questions on movies, personalities, family, restaurants, holiday can be asked provided you are sure that they are a *safe topic*. For example, family is considered a safe topic while talking to an Indian, and not so for a German.

We were at a client location in Europe closing a consultancy project. The client was very happy with the project team and hosted a dinner for the consultants. While the dinner was on, the project manager decided to chit-chat with the client. A lady from the client side was hosting the dinner. After some talks with the lady, the project manager suddenly remembered that in some conversations during their work someone had mentioned a cat that this lady had as a pet. So taking a chance to take this conversation further, the project manager asked: 'How is your pet cat?' The lady suddenly turned red and was seemingly upset and angry with the project manager, and said, 'How dare you ask me about her?' She excused herself and moved to some other table.

Be careful about subjects that you may talk about. While a topic may be absolutely fine in your country to talk about, may not be in another.

The easiest way to drive a great conversation is to talk about things which the person likes the most. Games, eating out, restaurants, movies, theatre and the list could be endless. However, when you are talking to a stranger, the easiest thing is to ask for their name. Ensure that you hear the other person out when he/she is saying her name. In case you have not heard it or you are unsure about the pronunciation, please *re-ask*. It is better to say, 'I am sorry if I got your name correctly. But could you please say it again?' From the next conversation, address by the name. For example, 'It was wonderful talking to you, Sunil.'

Don't take a wild guess in case you have forgotten the name. Please ask the other person for the name in such cases. 'I am sorry, but I have forgotten your name.' Forgetting a name is okay as long as you are honest about it. You may be meeting someone after years and it is possible to forget. The best thing to do in such situations is to walk up to the person, say a 'hello' and start conversing first by asking for their name. The worst, of course, is looking at the ground or trying to talk on your cell phone to suggest that you did not see the other person. Trying to avoid embarrassment or are not being interested in talking to the other person are both equally bad.

The challenges could be with difficult uncommon names or names of people of foreign origin. Spend some time learning the names. Do not forget them. As a leader, host or a manager, you must remember all of them by their names. Never look at the badges to know the names in case you have forgotten. Ask them again. Another essential aspect is not to call another person with their nick names or create nick names. 'Siddharth' does not become 'Sid' or 'Prasad Shukla Rao' does not become 'PISRO'. Never distort a name. Calling people with their names gives a feeling of acknowledgement and sincerity.

Jis took me out for a sales call after I joined as a management trainee. Jis walked into the reception of the office of a prospective client.

The receptionist was busy on the phone. After she completed, Jis engaged himself in a small talk with her:

Jis: So Jyotsna how are you?

Receptionist: Doing well. So you are here to meet boss? He is busy (checks with his secretary).

Jis: Why will I come here otherwise? You guys are not giving me a job offer these days.

Receptionist: (smiling) this is your company. Start working any time.

After some chit-chat about their business….

Jis: So how is your kid doing? Has she started going to school? Is she growing up to be naughty?

Receptionist: She is doing great Jis. Thanks for asking. She is really becoming naughty.

After some more time Jis asked the receptionist to check if the boss had gotten free. She walked from her seat, went to the boss directly and came back.

Receptionist: Now you have the permission to go and meet him.

Jis: Thank you for helping us meet him quickly.

They exchanged a smile and we went into the boss's room for a conversation.

After we walked out from the office I asked Jis about the meeting. He said, 'I started from where we had left the last time. I remember the last time I was meeting her, she was back to office after giving birth to a new-born baby.' Jis also gave me the most important lesson. Always start from where you had left. If you know their friends and families, start asking about them. This is living good memories.

HOW TO OPEN AND WHEN TO LEAVE?

The first step is to identify the right set of people to talk to. There are no right or wrong people, unless you want to speak to someone specifically. You might initially find it difficult to break in a conversation. Therefore, as a beginner, you should first look at people who are sitting alone. They could be eating their lunch or drinking their juice alone at the table. Another bet are the people with whom you have an 'eye contact'. In case you have an eye contact, grab the opportunity to smile back. You can then walk up to the person and start talking. In such situations, more open statements such as 'What brings you here', 'Wonderful arrangements out here' or the 'Food has been great' could start off a talk. In situations where you are all for the same purpose, like a dealers meet, find out topics of common interest. For example, 'How has been your journey so far?' The easiest way is to find a common ground. Finding a common ground or just taking a chance to talk is enough. While you may not be able to strike a chord with everyone, it would not be impossible to find out people who are willing to reciprocate. That is more than enough.

We also often tend to group with people who have similar interests or behaviours. For example, in a seminar with academicians and practitioners, people into research come together leaving the industry personnel in a different group. Try and break these barriers. These barriers are often due to our personal inhibitions. Our gender, culture, lifestyle, occupation often become a barrier to such small talks.

While you may be in the midst of speakers who genuinely show interest while you start talking to them, there will be others who would not be keen. Do not treat them as your failures. They are not. In fact, this could be because of many reasons such as a pre-occupied mind or a sense of urgency of the person. They could be completely different when you meet them otherwise. So a person who has refused to talk or has displayed cold shoulder once, should not be construed as their final opinion.

Your entry and exit to a talk, should appear pleasant. You might need to meet someone else in the room or check on the other stalls in an industrial fair. While the reasons for exit could be many, there are ways you can make the exit comfortable. Spend some considerable, quality time with each person. The simplest and easiest way to exit is to be upfront and honest. But, if you think that 'This conversation is rather turning out to be very boring' or going 'nowhere', then a part of the responsibility lies with you. Therefore, exit only when it is genuinely required or the purpose of starting the conversation is over. For example, you want to meet some of your customers or have to meet the chief guest whom you would want to invite in the future. You can say in such occasions, 'It was wonderful meeting you, Ravi. Can we catch some other time? I would also want to meet a couple of other people' (exchange your visiting cards, in case you have not). Ensure that you meet the other people immediately after that. Be honest and true to yourself and the other person from whom you have excused yourself. Another way of exiting from talks is to ask for a referral. 'Ravi, do you know the person who is sitting in the front row? I heard him talk and would want him to be invited to our organization.' In such situations, Ravi would either say a yes or a no. If it is a yes, take his help in meeting the new person. If it is a no, at least Ravi knows that you are now moving to the next speaker. You can also say, 'Ravi, would it be okay, if I can go ahead and talk to X?' The answer would invariably be a yes. In any exit, be honest. Another subtle way to exit a conversation is to introduce a third person. 'Ravi, have you met our new intern, Sushma?' You call her and introduce them, while you exit. Exit with honesty, graciousness and appreciation. For example, 'Thank you for meeting' or 'It was wonderful meeting you, Ravi' or 'Appreciate your time in talking to me and sharing your opinion.' If you want to follow this up with further meeting, you can always say, 'Why don't we catch up sometime when you are free? (exchange your contact details)'.

I was invited to talk to a bunch of new hires in our office. After my talk was over, one of them (Joy) came over and said:

Joy: I have seen you somewhere earlier.

Me: Are you sure?

Joy: Are you from Kolkata?

Me: Yes. I am from New Alipore in Kolkata.

Joy: Yes, I stay in the same place.

After a minute or two, I find out that he stays in the next apartment. After sometime, I asked him:

Me: So, where did you do your schooling from?

Joy: In Hare school.

Me: Do you know Mr Roshan Basu?

Joy: He was our math's teacher. I used to take coaching from him.

Me: He is my father-in-law.

I later checked that we had many such similarities.

Small talks can turn out to be very interesting. They brings out new dimensions in people and build connectivity.

While we discussed about situations when you would want to make an exit, there could be similar situations when the other person would want an exit. In such situations, you should be graceful enough to offer them an exit. A thank you at exit or being gracious to the other person is an emblem of your personality. End the talk with, 'It was lovely talking to you.' In case he would want the conversation to be taken ahead, he would exchange his card or share his contact details with you. Exit by the other party has a valid reason. Before an exit, they will display signs of their disinterest. A poor body language, little eye contact, fidgeting, looking around, asking very little questions or a disinterest in responses like a single-worded response to all open-ended questions you ask would suggest an exit. In such situations, give him a chance to exit gracefully.

To summarize, if the small talk is boring or mundane, half of the responsibility is on you. Exit with honesty from a conversation. Ensure that the reason for exit is gracious enough without hurting the other person. Do what you have announced that you would be doing, while exiting from the talk. Appreciate and thank people before you exit.

SET THE BALL ROLLING

You have now started talking and exchanged your names. Probably you would have asked a question or two. The next step is to set the ball rolling. You do not thank and abruptly end the conversation here at this stage. The onus is on you to deliver and take this ahead. Open-ended questions can never be responded with shorter answers and therefore you roll the ball forward. Typical stereotypes such as 'How is it going?', 'How was your weekend?' and 'How was your vacation?' have all the chances of a dead end. A one-word answer will kill it all. Therefore, in situations when you get a one-word reply, probe a little further. For example, 'How was your weekend?' and they say, 'Great'. You again ask, 'So what did you do? Did you get a chance to watch the football match?' This will drive it further. The essence here is to dig through. Ensure you do not cross the finer lines and cultural boundaries. Never discuss topics that are sensitive unless the other person brings up the topic. For example, asking about a divorce. Few cultures reserve some of the topics as personal and people are not keen on opening up.

You need a great amount of sincerity to set the ball rolling ahead and to give the person in front of you a fair chance to talk. If at any time the person in front feels connected, you are done. At this stage still many may not still be opening up. If you therefore see any signs of their possible exit, give them a fair chance to do so.

Another easy way of taking small talks ahead is using cues from a response. For example, you ask someone, 'So what did you do this weekend?' and he replies, 'Was watching European Premier League. The last time I visited Italy, I saw this craze for football.' By now you have four things to talk to him: his weekend, football, European Premier League or his visit to Italy.

If you are meeting someone after a long time, the easiest way to set the ball rolling is to start from where you had left. At a college reunion, the best way is to start is back from college days. If you meet certain people once every year, then the best way to start is, 'How is it different this year?' or 'You look different from last year?'

Acquaintances are the easiest bet. You know them and it is easy to roll the ball forward. However, ensure that you do not hang on for long. While you exchange pleasantries, take the conversation ahead and exit to meet new people. Ensure that you are not too quick nor too late.

One of our customers was not renewing his advertisement. My sales executive was following up with him for quite some time. One day he gave up on this customer and asked me to join the sales call. I went with him for this call.

When we were sitting with our customer, his phone rang. I overheard the conversation about a consignment of cheese that he had imported.

I diverted the conversation on purpose.

Me: So by any chance do you deal with cheese?

Him: Yes, we deal with all kinds of cheese.

Me: So where is your store?

Him: My store is in Gurgaon.

Me: So what kind of cheese do you store? Do you have Brie, Camembert, Gouda, Gorgonzola, Roquefort and Stilton?

Him: (After looking at me for a few seconds) How do you know?

Me: Cheese is fascinating. Although in India we do not have a culture of eating cheese, France does.

Him: (Looks at me with further curiosity).

We keep talking about cheese for the next half an hour. I had forgotten the purpose for which I had come. My sales executive gave me a small knock below the table to get me back.

After some time, I convinced him to renew the existing advertisement. He did. I then asked him, 'Why don't you take a look at the category of cheese and place an advertisement as well. I doubt whether in our city people know that there is a cheese store which deals with such fine quality cheese.'

He got convinced. He placed a second advertisement in the cheese category as well.

Another way of rolling the talk ahead is to look at symbols. A badge on the table, a coffee mug with an emblem, a family photo, t-shirt with a logo, books on the table or a club membership. All these could be used as a mechanism to roll the ball forward. For example, asking, 'I saw you receiving books in the mail today? So what did you order for?'

An important aspect of great small talks is listening. We will take a look at the importance of listening in the following chapters. Remember that talking and listening go hand in hand. You cannot keep on talking, otherwise the conversation will end. When a person talks, a natural tendency of human brains and minds is to digress from the track. Our minds run away from listening. Even before you come back to the discussion, you realize that a large part of the talk is over. Therefore, during small talks, listen and not just hear. Be sincere while talking and listening. If you are, your body language would automatically turn positive. The true signs that a person is listening can be judged by his non-verbal cues, such as leaning forward, eye contact, nodding, smiling, asking questions and paraphrasing. This would come automatically if you are sincere while listening. If you are disingenuous or reluctant, then do not take a talk ahead. Exit. Enter only when you are willing to do so.

WHAT NOT TO DO IN A SMALL TALK?

Now that we have discussed on how to start, set the ball rolling and how to end, it is now time to talk about some don'ts in a small talk. First, of course, is to shoot questions one after another. It puts off the other person as he may feel as if he is being treated as a prisoner of war, brought in front of the execution squad, which is why it is a big no. Second to ask questions which are sensitive, such as miscarriage, pregnancy, divorce and ill health. The third is to brag about yourself.

If you keep talking about the same thing repeatedly, you become predictable, especially to people who know you well. Stop blowing your own trumpet. The fourth is 'rushing with your own version of the story'. In some conversations, while others are talking about a particular incident, you rush in with what happened to you in a similar circumstance and hijack. It leaves the other person feeling worse than what he already did. The fifth is to gossip in small talk. If others are, excuse yourself or do not participate.

We are what we say and that is what makes conversations and small talk critical. Use these as very effective tools in building and nurturing your relationship with people, inside and outside the organization.

BIBLIOGRAPHY

1. Debra Fine, *The Fine Art of Small Talk: How to Start a Conversation, Keep It Going, Build Networking Skills—And Leave a Positive Impression!* (New York, NY: Hyperion, 2005).

6 Give Your Mouth a Break: Listen!!!

*I remind myself every morning: Nothing I say
this day will teach me anything. So if I'm going to learn,
I must do it by listening.*

—Larry King

WHY LISTEN TO PEOPLE?

The following are famous lines by Bill Marriott, Executive Chairman of the Marriott International.

> I'm often asked the question, 'What's the most important skill for great leadership?' And I always have the same answer—listening. In a service industry, you have to listen to your employees and your customers. Listening allows us all to learn what our guests are looking for in a stay, what's important to them and their likes and dislikes.[1]

Be it interacting with your customers or speaking to your colleagues, the importance of listening is paramount. For every role in business or life, you need to listen; and we spend about 50 per cent of our time in listening to people.

When I was in school, the principal came in one day and said, 'I will ask you a question. Let me see who can answer this right.' The

---

[1] Bill Marriot, 'We Are Always Listening,' Marriot Blog, 19 October 2010, https://www.blogs.marriott.com/marriott-on-the-move/2010/10/we-are-always-listening.html (accessed on 26 May 2019).

question she asked was: 'You are driving a bus. Ten people get on the bus, then seven get down at the next stop and four get in the next and six get down. What is the age of the bus driver?' We started calculating and rethinking on the question. My batchmates had different answers. But no one had the correct answer.

Listening is an involuntary activity. While communicating, we exchange a lot of messages, understand and summarize our thoughts as well as others'. However, this skill set is highly underrated and not handled well by people. Although we have two ears and one mouth, we talk more than we listen to people. In a study done by Ralph G. Nichols and Leonard A. Stevens, respondents were amazed to find out that first, 80 per cent of the work of an individual is dependent on listening. Second a lot of troubles brew in the work environments as a result of not listening to people. Third although listening is one of the most important faces of communication, it has been overlooked.

The importance and impact of effective listening is enormous. On the one hand you have the customers and on the other there are employees. For every corporation the objective is to have a set of satisfied customers achieved through their employee base. To achieve this, we need to have a satisfied employee base. It is therefore critical for employees to listen to their customers, and companies to their employees and customers. This will strengthen organizational relationships, and build a better work environment and a sense of bonding. Listening nurtures innovation and manages diversity. Listening ensures that you are not losing foothold in the marketplace or your employees.

In the year 1909, (2 July) Akhil Chandra Sen, a traveller of the erstwhile British Railways in India, wrote this letter to the Transportation Superintendent of the Sahibganj divisional railway office.

'Dear Sir,

I am arrive by passenger train Ahmedpur station and my belly is too much swelling with jackfruit. I am therefore went to privy. Just I doing the nuisance that guard making whistle blow for train to go off and I am running with lotah in one hand and dhoti in the next when I am fall over and expose all my shocking to man and female women on platform. I am got leaved at Ahmedpur station. This too much bad, if passenger go to make dung that dam guard not wait train five minutes for him. I am therefore pray your honor to make big fine on that guard for public sake. Otherwise I am making big report to papers.'

While this letter might not be grammatically correct, but as a customer of the railways, he mattered. The letter changed the way railways ran. They introduced 'toilets' in the trains for the first time, though passenger trains had been in India since 1853.[2]

Missing luggage is a part of any airport or airline. This is because of the massive cargo that is handled at international airports. Dave Carroll was traveling to Nebraska for a one-week musical tour in 2008 and his guitar was broken by the airline staff of United Airlines. Dave alleged that he heard a fellow passenger claim that baggage handlers at the Chicago O'Hare International Airport threw a guitar during a layover on his flight from Halifax Stanfield International Airport to Omaha. Dave tried everything to get a fair compensation. The guitar costed the singer $3500. The airlines had not denied the same, but even after nine months of follow up the airline company did not pay back a single dollar back to Dave for his guitar. The claim was denied because the airline company said that the complaint was not made within the stipulated '24 hours' time.

After being denied, he promised that he would write three songs and post them on YouTube. The result was that the song 'United Breaks Guitars', the first of the three song became a sensation. It surpassed millions of views in a span of weeks. With social media in action, United immediately offered him compensation, but it was too late.

This is the power of listening or not listening.

---

[2] Akash Deep Ashok, 'When Using a Train Toilet, Thank Okhil Babu for His Hilarious Letter,' *India Today*, 12 February 2014, https://www.indiatoday.in/india/north/story/indian-railways-history-160-years-interesting-facts-180735-2014-02-12 (accessed on 26 May 2019).

Communication ties every stakeholder in business and more of it lies in the spoken words than the written words. While spoken words are important and what we say is critical, but the effectiveness lies in how we listen.

LEAD BY LISTENING: HOW LISTENING CAN HELP US?

Most of the successful people I've known are the ones who do more listening than talking.

—Bernard Baruch

Sajina came into the room of her boss, (Raj) while I was sitting with him. Sajina, does not report to me, but I have known her for quite some time. Her boss, annoyed, asked her, 'Have you completed the work that I had given you?' She was quiet with her head down. Her boss was even more annoyed. Her boss said, 'Either you do this by the end of the day or leave this company and permanently go back home. Enough of this.' Sajina kept quiet and walked out of the room.

After she walked out, Raj asked me, 'What do you do with such people. What will you call such people?' I said, 'Inefficient'. Raj stopped me and said, 'Inefficient is an inappropriate word. The right words for her are callousness, idiotic, useless and many more.'

However, something stopped me from believing this. I had known Sajina for quite some time and my understanding of her was different from what I saw and what Raj made me believe. Although she did not report to me, I called her out for a coffee. She was reluctant, but finally she agreed. She did not want to speak up (as I was a close friend of Raj) and after a lot of dilly-dallying she spoke.

'My family issues are not allowing me to focus on my work. Half of my mind is at home and half at work. I am going through a rough marriage, parents are unwell at home and there is no one to take care of my kid. My parents are just managing with the small pension that they get and there is no one to support us. My salary is being used for their medicines and there is little left for my kid. It is pathetic managing all of these. I do not know if I should be alive.'

This hit me real hard. I took some time out and helped her out of this. I also spoke to Raj and ensured that she is treated with some liberty till she settles down.

So as I stopped to think on what went wrong in her meeting with Raj, I realized that the problem was with Raj and me. We jumped to a conclusion. Raj had created a mental barrier with some pieces of information from her past action, arranged them conveniently, and jumped to a conclusion with some hard hitting words explaining her action. This mental barrier and the filter prevented him from seeing her from the right perspective.

Summarizing it: 'We did not listen to her in the first instance.'

Inherently and naturally we do not listen. So is it that I am not listening? Absolutely you are and are not...You are either hearing or selectively listening. Hearing as a process is not the same as listening. Hearing is a natural function of the ear, which means the reception of a sound. The ear is your sensory organ. Listening, however, is acquired, which involves understanding of the messages in communication.

Listening helps you to: Get the relevant information, gain by sharing the knowledge and experiences of others, and help people resolve the challenges. Organizations take decisions on the feedback given. The feedback gives critical inputs to the running of the business. Listening better would help you make better and faster decisions. In the case of Sajina, had Raj really listened, there could have been other ways of tackling the problem. The easiest way would have been to divide her work which would have made it easier for both of them. Listening improves the flow of communication, making it more open and receptive. Higher receptivity would translate into higher motivation for the people. When you are heard in the organization, you are in the process of building stronger relationships. Listening helps in improving productivity and it helps nurture creativity at work. As an individual, listening helps to: Understand the work and people better, be efficient, have better relationships with stakeholders and manage customers better. A study done by Guy Itzchakov and Avraham published in *Harvard Business Review* says that listening helps in making a person feel relaxed, being self-aware about their strengths and weaknesses, and more willing to reflect in a non-defensive manner. They cooperate more than competing, and share their ideas and attitudes with people rather than persuading others to follow their ideas. They are also more open to ideas and different point of views.[3]

Listening forms an essential part in the work dynamics, and is an acquired skill which is different from hearing. Listening is an important skill which you must acquire. Thought leaders such as Stephen Covey and Dale Carnegie have focused on the most important aspect of listening, that is, to build, enhance and nurture relationships. Waggl, for example, researched 500,000 business leaders. They asked if listening to their employees and incorporating their ideas is critical success factors for organizational success, a 97 per cent responded affirmatively.[6]

WHAT'S THE CATCH: WHAT STOPS US FROM LISTENING?

> Most people do not listen with the intent to understand; they listen with the intent to reply.
>
> —Stephen R. Covey

It is our preconceived notions, ideas and prejudices about people that prevent us from listening. We are standing with our experiences and perceptions about people every time a new thinking is formed over an old one. For example, you are repairing a road. You will put the tar on the old road. Rarely will you scrape the old tar to build a new road completely. Our human brains also work in the same way. The

---

[3] Guy Itzchakov and Avraham N. (Avi) Kluger, 'The Power of Listening in Helping People Change', *Harvard Business Review*, 17 May 2018, https://hbr.org/2018/05/the-power-of-listening-in-helping-people-change; (accessed on 26 May 2019).

new tar is laid on the old one. Our judgements about people are quite similar because they draw heavily from the past, especially interactions and similar experiences. While in some cases they may not prove to be wrong, they may not be right either, as in our example above. So it is your prejudices that shape your thoughts and while this is natural, this may not be right. These will keep on hitting us for quite some time and this will distort our thought process and our ability to listen.

Listening is inhibited by two things. First is our *inability to listen,* second is *when the environment around is not conducive to listening.*

The employees of a company received an email form HR (teaser mail) that an auto driver 'Annadurai' would be coming to their office to speak about customer relationship management (CRM). The same evening, during tea, one of the employees said, 'Who is this guy? What can we learn from an auto driver? Does the HR not have any other better job than bringing him to our office?' On the day of the session, the auditorium was packed to the brim. People were standing to listen to him. People who had decades of experience in CRM had come to hear him. He drove an auto in Chennai and is a six-time TEDx speaker. His auto is booked by Indians and foreigners for the next eight months. Even head of states, prime ministers have booked and travelled in his auto.

Our inability to listen is because of our selective perception and perceptual distortion. While selective perception is about listening to selective things, the latter is about interpreting it the way we want to or the way our minds are conditioned to. For example, when the head of sales is talking about the yearly performance of the sales team, you tend to focus only on things that matter to you the most, for example, the rewards and recognitions to be announced or the incentives planned and so on. Your mind suitably skips the remaining information. The perceptual distortion will come into action because of your pre-conceived notion about people. Even if the sales head is talking good about the sales team, you keep telling yourself, 'Full year you all have blasted us, now the targets have been met, you are showering your affection' or 'Useless guy...Never has anything good to say.' Even if the person makes sense, you block it because of your earlier perceptions.

Our inability to listen could also be because of our disinterest, that is, when you feel that you already know about it or when you feel that it is irrelevant for you as a person. The first is a 'know it all attitude' and the second is demonstrating the behaviour of a turtle, which hides in his shell on the sight of any danger around him. The *know it all attitude* happens frequently with educationists and trainers. The moment the participant asks a question, the trainer is ready with his answer, even before the question is over. While this may be termed as 'experience', we are often on the wrong foot. The second is when people shun themselves to listening. Questions such as 'What is in it for me?' and 'Why should I?' start coming in your mind even before the speaker has started talking. This blocks our ability and willingness to listen. Even if something good has been said, the mind will be reluctant to capture any information thereon. A stressed mind is another reason for our unwillingness to listen.

Sugandha was my reportee. She was due for her promotion. I congratulated her and told her that she may get an email any time soon during the day from HR. Next day, she came to me and said, 'I have not received an email from the HR about my promotion.' I called up the HR and verified. They confirmed that the email has been sent. After a lot of brainstorming, someone asked me to ask her to check her junk folder. The email was found in the junk folder. I asked Sugandha, 'Why did the HR mail land in the junk folder?' She said, 'I had set a rule that HR mails must be moved to the junk folder.' I asked, 'But why?' She replied, 'Most of their mails are rubbish. They do not matter to me.' This is what hinders us from listening; our preconceived notions.

The environment around us is the second biggest barrier that hinders us from listening.

For example, a long telephonic conversation might be difficult. Other environment related barriers would be chatting, talking loudly on phone amongst others. Improper seating arrangement, poor ventilation and even the timing can act as a barrier to listening. Imagine listening to someone in a meeting where the mobile phones rang thrice, someone checked his messages, couple of people around you were responding to their emails and some of them went to pick up their coffee even before the break was announced.

Rajat had gone to train a large group of people. The training sessions required a lot of interaction. However, owing to the paucity of time and space, three hundred people attended the program together. Rajat was unhappy with this and on the first day he told this to the organizers. On the last day, many people came back with the feedback that they were not able to gather anything from the training. The organizers tried to put this on Rajat. He denied accepting any responsibility. He said, 'I knew this would happen. You cannot do a training for a topic like this for a three hundred people audience. No one would be able to gather anything out of it.'

In another case, Rajat was asked to present a set of initiatives taken up in his department to prospective Middle East-based new clients. It was a Friday. He was given a time slot before lunch. Barely had he started talking that the clients looked at their watches and said, 'It is a Friday and you will have to excuse us for our prayers.' Rajat waited and post lunch he was informed that the meeting got cancelled as there were something more important that the clients had to attend to.

Rajat went to a B-school to give a talk on the importance of communication and what is in store for the new generation business managers. Each session had 120 people and the room was poorly lit. The room was rectangular in shape with the audio not working properly. If Rajat had to talk to someone at the back of the room, he had to either walk up to the end or raise his voice. There were three sessions packed during the day. While he managed the first two sessions, the third session had a poor feedback. Rajat had drained all his energy talking very loudly in the first two sessions and managing such a large audience.

We speak at about 150 words per minute, but think at 600 words per minute. Therefore, this gives the mind a lot of vacant spots which makes it wander. The attention span of people is getting lower and it is a normal behaviour for the brain to take that 'break'. This explains the mental absence of the listeners and it results into 'selective listening'. Another set of listeners get engrossed in challenging what is being spoken about either to challenge the speaker or test his knowledge, and his focus moves to what he needs to speak. They are self-centred listeners. We also do not listen because we were never taught to. In school and college, we had courses on writing, speaking and reading. Listening was missing and that is also what makes us very poor listeners. A study done by Ralph G. Nichols and Leonard A. Stevens, found out that our assumption that listening ability depends largely on intelligence and that 'bright' people listen well and 'dull' ones poorly is wrong. Also learning to read will also teach us to listen is also another false assumption that we all make.[4]

Listening as a process is very complex. Listeners assume. If you have been talking to an audience and after making a couple of statements ask them to repeat, you will be surprised to see that how people have misinterpreted what you have said. Just think about the silly questions that people ask after you have said them something.

A trainee reporter came rushing to an aeroplane waiting at the airport. The pilot was waiting. The reporter rushed in and said, 'Let's go.' The pilot started off and flew up in the sky. The trainee reporter told the pilot, 'Can you please fly a little low over this particular area? (pointing to the map).' The pilot asked, 'But why?' The reporter said, 'I am covering the flood in that area.' The pilot said, 'Aren't you my flying instructor?'

Our listening is greatly inhibited by our emotions and our past beliefs. If we strongly believe in something, we will be unwilling to listen to anything 'right' that is being said. The most common example is when you adore or follow a sporting star or a political party, anything written against that person is shunned by you. You neither want to read, hear nor listen to anything negative about them. This is primarily because of the emotions that play. Even if someone is saying things which are logical and factual, you will find every other excuse to side by your emotions.

Our past beliefs also have a role to play. If we had a particular experience with a colleague at our office, (good/bad) it is very difficult to get that off our mind. It sticks very strongly to us and we base our listening on it. We will find everything that will approve/disapprove our past belief.

Deepak was a sales executive working for a firm. He had a strategy that he never used to push his customers to close the deal. He used to leave the customers open and would wait for them to turn around with their proposal. This was not liked by the sales manager. He was of the opinion that pushing the customers was necessary. This created a discord and the sales manager started disliking Deepak although he was reasonably good with his sales. It later came to a stage when the sales manager was unwilling to hear anything that was spoken about him in any meetings. He used to shoo away anything positive that was being said about him.

TYPES OF LISTENING

> One of the most sincere forms of respect is actually listening to what another has to say.
>
> —Bryant H. McGill

As a listener, you must first understand the type of listening. This helps you gel with the situation.

Content Listening: Listening to the Untold Story

First is *content listening*, that is, when you are listening to gather information or to learn something or keeping yourself abreast of a situation.

'Our sales performance for the last financial year has been good, with the overall operating margins improving by 10 per cent year-on-year.' 'We have been able to retain about 90 per cent of our existing clients. The sales figures have improved in almost all the regions except for pockets in down south and some regions in the east. For the western regions the sales were mostly muted, with sales from key clients marginally increasing or decreasing.'

You hear these on a daily basis while you talk to your manager or colleague. Never be judgmental about them. Hear them as if you are trying to garner information. However, the moment you start analysing it while it is being said, you are getting sidetracked from just listening to the content. So when do you analysing? Only if you need to. Else do not analyse such information. The analysis must be kept post the listening. Three things that will guide you through this. First focus on what is being said, second critically do not examine such content and third listen to the message as a source of information. Never challenge the speaker. You are being counter-productive as the information you gather is rarely going to help you. However, you may ask questions or clarify your doubts.

Empathic Listening: Listen with Your Heart

Second is *empathic listening*, that is, trying to understand the feelings of the speaker without any prejudices.

After the appraisal cycle got over, Sneha came to me and said, 'I do not know why I am spending my efforts in this company. A useless organization with another set of useless managers leading the company. There are no parameters that define our roles and responsibilities and the promotions are ad-hoc.

Look at Ravi? Do you think this guy even deserves a promotion?'

In this type of listening you listen to the speaker with empathy. However, it does not mean that you support or disapprove his/her ideas. You are giving a patient hearing to the person sitting right in front of you, showing concern. While it may be wrong at this stage to provide advice unless specifically asked for; many people may come to you to air their grievances or share a piece of good news. You should keep yourself open in such circumstances. Handling such situations could be tricky as some of these listening may make you to take a side. Refrain from taking sides, especially if you possess a different viewpoint from what is being said. To guide you through this type, first make the person comfortable. Show your concern and be genuinely interested. Second clarify and support verbally as well as non-verbally. Your questions and summarizing should do the bit. Third refrain from advising in such situations. In case you are forced to, handle such situations with diplomacy. For example, pose a question as an answer, 'So what you think you should be doing?' or 'What will be your next step?' or 'Don't you think this will be something very rude coming from you as a person?'

Evaluative Listening: Listening with the Mind

Last is *evaluative listening or critical listening*, that is, trying to judge the intentions of the person or the content. Realize that all the three types are different and the approach you adopt would differ. Therefore, the first step is to be conscious about the type of listening that you are going to do.

The financial year was not great and the sales head had called for a meeting. The meeting was to hear the viewpoints of his managers to 'meet' the targets for the year and to strategize. While the discussion was going on, a group of managers raised their voices on increasing the productivity of people. Another group asked the sales head to trim down the non-productive people as they were neither contributing anything and were pulling down the morale of the others who were performing. The sales manager heard them for quite some time and reserved his opinion for the next meeting.

In this type of listening you are judging the person along with what you are listening to. Be wary about adequacy and factual correctness of the information presented. In evaluative listening many people try and take the emotional aspect of a topic and get along deliberating on the positive feelings, underplaying the negative or vice-versa. Be wary of such people. In such listening first ask questions, second take detailed notes or have the minutes in place and third evaluate the pros and cons of both sides before the final decision-making. Ensure that you have validated what has been said and treaded cautiously on what has been presented or said. Ask questions if necessary.

BECOMING A BETTER LISTENER

> Wisdom is the reward you get for a lifetime of listening when you'd have preferred to talk.
>
> —Doug Larson

To become a better listener is probably the most difficult of all and requires very hard work. It requires tremendous amount of practice, and even great speakers or the ones who are great with their abilities to write or win hearts through their talks fail when it comes to their listening abilities. This happens primarily on multiple accounts. While we have discussed the barriers, let us try and understand this with some depth. Our brains have tremendous processing capabilities. Right from our childhood the brain has been synchronizing all our thoughts into action. You first think and it results into an action. For example, you want to pick up a book. The brain thinks first and then the arms lift it up. There is a signal from the brain to your arms which results into this action. So when we listen, we listen to the words which the speaker is saying at a rate of 120 per minute. However, your brain is processing thoughts much faster than those spoken words. Therefore, you are riding a jet and the speaker is on a bullock cart. The person on the bullock cart will never be able to catch you. You will need to consciously slow down your thought process to catch the bullock cart. You *therefore need plenty of concentration.* While the speaker is saying something, your mind is working faster. While it is fast, it tries to do two things. First it conveniently drives you out to something more convenient, which does not have any logic or something which you may want to desperately tell the speaker. Second it merges some of the thoughts of the speaker with your own and you find it difficult to apprehend later which was the right version. The end is disastrous. You would not even have listened to a major chunk of what had been said. Also the time the mind wanders is also not in your control. So you may have lost out hearing either a major chunk, a minor portion or pieces of it, depending on how long your mind was wondering around.

So what do you do in such situations? These are some of the things that you should practice.

First: Concentrate while listening. While this is the most difficult part, concentrating in an age of distractions is a difficult proposition. The easiest thing to do is to switch off your mobile phones, laptops or any other digital or electronic instruments around you. Sit away from people who know you (if you can). In that way you will be disturbed less. You can also inform your colleagues not to bother you for a specified time. Focus on your mind to create a model of what is being said. You may draw pictures to retain the information or arrange the abstract concepts in a way that helps you retain. When you are listening for longer durations, focus on the key words and phrases. Avoid multi-tasking, especially drafting emails while listening or taking phone calls while talking (unless very important ones).

Second: Think and feel with the speaker. While the speaker is talking, start thinking in terms of what is being said. Summarize the things said mentally. Apprehend what is the next thing that he could probably say or the things he has omitted. Here you can also focus on checking if the speaker has provided enough indication of what has been said.

You also need to feel with the speaker. When you are engrossed watching a movie, you start living the protagonist of the movie. Likewise, for someone whom you are listening to, live the speaker and feel what is being said. If the speaker is narrating something about fear or joy, live it and feel it with empathy. Think what would have happened if you had been there at that time.

Taking notes at various stages also keeps you glued to the speaker. You may also want to write down the doubts you have or questions that come to your mind. However, remember the type of listening. The type will determine the strategy that you will primarily adopt.

Third: Be choosy with what you really need to listen. Our time is limited. We need to ration it out for various activities. At the organization, if we keep spending our time listening to things that really would not/don't matter, then we are wasting our time. However, do not get me wrong. I am not against listening, but pick and choose the ones you need to listen. So how do you choose the ones? This is a difficult question to answer. Measure it on avoidability and importance. If it is unavoidable but important, fix it first. If it is avoidable and unimportant, handle it last or postpone it. However, if you have committed to listening, put your soul into it. Remember that listening is not easy. It severely taxes our mind and body. Greater the amount of listening that you do, the more exhausted you will feel. Imagine sitting daylong for business meetings. It is taxing both for the mind and body.

Fourth: Be genuinely interested in listening to people. Make the other person feel 'felt'. Do not wait for your turn to drive down your point. If the other person feels 'valued' after talking to you, you have been successful. To become a great leader your people must have sufficient trust on you and this somewhere is built on the premises of good listening abilities.

Our department had become 'headless' after my boss retired. So the de facto responsibility to own everything went to the next-in-command, Mani, although she was never 'officially' designated as the head. The organization had been going through a rough time and there was a lot of chaos in the system owing to a re-fitment exercise that had happened. Our roles were being re-fitted into a new system that the organization had developed as a restructuring exercise. However, like any other change, there was chaos bound in such system, especially when the organisation is huge in size. There was a lot of apprehension among people during that time as many people felt that they were getting demoted as a result of this exercise. I was one of them. The problem became a nightmare especially because we did not have anyone who could lend us their ears, especially without a head around who could take up our cases.

So I approached Mani, like many others in our team, and I explained to her why the current fitment was not apt in my case. I said that in case the fitment is done forcefully, I would have no other option but to start looking for new opportunities. She listened to me carefully and asked me to prepare a small case on why I feel that I should be moved to a higher fitment in the hierarchy on the basis of my experience. She took up my case with the senior management and patiently detailed out everything that I had to say to the higher ups. The higher ups were convinced and fitted me to a higher role. I owed a lot to Mani for this. Had she simply refused to take this up or had dilly-dallied because she was not the head, I would have miserably lost out a couple of years of my experience. Only because of her I got my position right after this exercise. My respect for Mani went up manifold times after this, especially her ability to listen to people and take action.

FROM LISTENING TO ACTIONIZING

> There is a difference between listening and waiting for your turn to speak.
>
> —Simon Sinek

You would have understood by now that listening is not an easy task. Although essential, we are not trained to handle this. It is now time for you to start becoming a great listener because you cannot do away with this essential skill of communicating.

Action 1: Appreciate that listening is not easy. It will take months or probably years of effort to change your old habits. You must practice as much as you can consciously to become a listener. Remember the 80–20 Pareto Principle. Listen for 80 per cent of the time and speak for another 20 per cent.

Action 2: While we are listening, it is inherent in our nature to criticize either the content or the speaker. This could happen when either the speaker is younger to you or you are listening to something which you do not understand. Your efforts should not be to undermine the speaker or what he has worn for that day, but on listening to him.

Stop criticizing the speaker or his content, and try and gather as much as you can. Start listening to things that are varied. You might not be interested in politics, but can you listen to a political debate, provided it is not eating up your time?

Action 3: Multi-tasking and listening do not go hand in hand. Sometime senior managers get calls while you might be discussing something critical with them. So it happens with you. Listening is a standalone activity. It cannot be done with anything else. If you do so, you will either lose the confidence of the speaker or lose out on important points the person is trying to say. Be present at the moment. Make eye contact with the person who is speaking to you.

Action 4: Our pre-conceived notions and our emotions are our biggest baggage in listening. These go hand in hand while we try to listen. If we have christened someone bad, he remains bad throughout unless your brain is reprogrammed to call him as good. When some speaks, leave the baggage out. Listen with an open mind and soul.

Action 5: Never judge the person sitting in front of you. This is the worst thing that you could be doing. You are not providing the person any solution. You will be wonderful if you can 'just' lend your ears to the person. We jump to conclusions and judgements based on similar events or acts that we have heard or seen. Your role as a listener is not to 'judge' but to empathize.

Action 6: You might love your voice, you might love your ideas and you might feel you are born to change the world with your ideas. Throw them out of the window while you listen because listening does not need any of these. Just because your idea is great does not mean you pitch your ideas or thrust them. Listening is not about thrusting ideas.

Action 7: If you have not understood, clarify. Ask questions but only to clarify. Many people while listening, try to ask intelligent questions to bother the speaker or test his intelligence. Sometimes they want to stand out of the crowd. Never do any of these. Only genuine doubts and things that need clarification should be asked.

Action 8: The speaker needs to be comforted. He needs to understand if he is going wrong or right. He needs to understand if you are able to grasp the subject. While listening give feedback. Ask questions like, 'Can you please repeat this idea to clarify?' Cooperate with the speaker by asking questions that help him gather confidence. Keeping silent kills the morale of a speaker.

Phew!!!!!That is a lot of work. Never thought listening to be so difficult. It is the most difficult aspect of communication and to be a great leader and a communicator this is a must-have skill. And I must say that I am still working on this. I end this echoing the thoughts of Lee Iacocca—CEO, Chrysler Corporation: 'I only wish I could find an institute that teaches people how to listen. Business people need to listen at least as much as they need to talk. Too many people fail to realize that real communication goes in both directions.'

BIBLIOGRAPHY

1. Ralph G. Nichols and Leonard A. Stevens, 'Listening to People', *Harvard Business Review*, September 1957, https://hbr.org/1957/09/listening-to-people (accessed on 26 May 2019).

2. Wikipedia, 'United Breaks Guitars', Wikipedia, https://en.wikipedia.org/wiki/United_Breaks_Guitars (accessed on 26 May 2019).

3. Waggl, '2016 Predictions for Human Capital Results,' Waggl Blog, 17 December 2015, https://www.waggl.com/blog/2015/12/17/2016-predictions-for-human-capital-results/ (accessed on 26 May 2019).

4. Mark Goulston, *Just Listen: Discover the Secret to Getting Through to Absolutely Anyone* (New York, NY: American Management Association, 2010).

7 Managing Difficult Conversations: Deal-Breakers to Makers

Everyone has their own ways of expression. I believe we all have a lot to say, but finding ways to say it is more than half the battle.

—Criss Jami

WHAT ARE DIFFICULT CONVERSATIONS?

Some communications are difficult, very difficult. In some cases you need to maintain a good relationship with the person or probably you have had a good relationship with the person for a long time. You know this person professionally as well as personally. In some other cases people start doing things that are beyond protocols or rules. Some things are difficult to talk about, such as harassment or bullying in an organization. There could be many such more. These conversations are not normal either for you to say or for the person in front of you to hear because it may not be the normal course of action. You could be taking the other person by surprise or the person listening to you may be taken aback by these conversations.

A study done by CMI shows that in UK the top three most dreaded conversations are related to work. They include pay, colleagues' inappropriate behaviour and feedback about poor performance.[1]

---

[1] https://www.managers.org.uk/insights/news/2015/july/the-10-most-difficult-conversations-new-surprising-research (accessed on 25 May 2019).

Rajat is the best sales guy in your team. He does extremely well and the entire office is proud of him. However, he hates to report the sales call data. The management mandates that every week a report be sent on how many sales call a person has made. Rajat, however, refuses to do this. His point is, 'How does that matter till business is coming? Ask me if I am unable to get you business.' Senior management wants the reports every week. You cut a sorry figure as his data is incomplete every time. You now need to give an ultimatum to Rajat.

Amit is becoming a nuisance at office. He takes confidential calls in his cubicle, talks loudly to others coming to meet him, talks rubbish with people, is always out of context, hijacks meetings and never gives due respect to his colleagues. He loves working in a silo, avoids his team members, does things as he feels and keeps repeating that his entire team is jealous and has ganged up against his growth. He has a 'know it all attitude'. Although his manager has tried to coach and mentor him, he has failed miserably. The entire team is complaining about his non-cooperation as their work gets stuck due to his lackadaisical attitude. The manager now needs to tell him, 'enough is enough'.

It is a difficult conversation when you have to say things which are correct, but are unpleasing for the listener to hear. For example, harassment or bullying. Sometimes difficult conversations could be with handling different types you people, who just drive you crazy. Something like, 'Oh God, please give this person some common sense. How long do I have to handle this person?' The biggest problem however is taking a harsh decision post a difficult conversation, such as firing or rejecting a long time vendor or not being able to give a promotion to your most eligible employee and so on. Sometimes you would have counselled/mentored/coached a person hundred times, but still he refuses to change. The 'toxic boss', the 'uncompassionate manager', 'know it all' colleague, the 'perfect' person, 'the flirty executive' and so on are all difficult conversations that you could handle. Sometimes difficult conversations are tough to anticipate and you really do not expect them coming. Take this example:

An employee was facing a gross charge of misconduct in his organization. It was investigated and found that some of the confidential documents were leaked by this employee. He was called by HR to have a discussion. The HR wanted to have a discussion with the employee before taking the final call. He came to meet them and barely after they started talking, the employee shouted, 'You all are responsible for this. It is my manager who has conspired against me and I am going to take an action against all of you. I will be committing suicide tonight with my wife and son and I will write a note, explaining this harassment and behaviour. I will also call the police before committing this suicide. Let me see who prevents you from going to jail.' After saying this he walks out of the room.

You wanted to have a difficult conversation, but now you feel helpless. The employee is threatening you, but now you cannot initiate an action against him.

Take another situation.

I was talking to the head of HR of a company, and I asked him, 'What is the most difficult conversation that you have ever had?' He said, 'When I joined my first job, I came into office one morning and my boss called me up. He said, "Ratan, one of your employees has died in a road accident. Please inform their family." I was shocked. I did not know what to tell and how to tell.

I called up the police station and found out that she was going for some official work to New Delhi. It was an early morning flight and on the way to the Bangalore airport, the driver slept off and crashed into a truck which was parked in a by-lane. Both the driver and the employee died on spot. I kept telling myself, what do I tell the family? How do I tell them that their daughter who had left home an hour back is no more?

It took me extreme courage to pick the phone and call them. Her father received the call. When I passed this message, there was absolute silence. I had become numb. Her father kept the phone down.'

Ratan concluded, 'Conveying messages about death to the family members and their loved ones was something which I always dreaded to do.'

WHY WE ARE BAD AT HANDLING DIFFICULT CONVERSATIONS?

> Conversation. What is it? A mystery! It's the art of never seeming bored, of touching everything with interest, of pleasing with trifles, of being fascinating with nothing at all.
>
> —Guy de Maupassant

This difficulty arises primarily because of two reasons. First is our inability to speak up. We fear speaking up. Second is the unwillingness or the inability to accept the message. The difference probably is in how we react. If someone tells us at office, 'This work has not been well done. I expected you to do better' or 'This is a horrible piece of work from you', you tend to take this personally. You do it more because the relationship in an organization is more impersonal and transactional. Had this relationship been with someone whom you had worked together for years, sharing a very good camaraderie, you would have adjusted yourself after listening to this message. Neither would the person saying it have an inhibition telling it nor the person listening to it. Similarly, if you have to confront such situations, we commonly follow three approaches. The first approach is, 'Sir, if you do not like my work, please let me know and I will start looking out.' The second approach is, 'Sir, you are a genius. Had I got a mentor like you, I would have reached the skies till now.' The third approach is to avoid confrontations. This category of people will remain silent and start searching for a new job or keep quiet, suffering silently. The first group are the 'hot headed' people, unwilling to listen or respond appropriately. They react. The second group of people are the 'boot-lickers' who find out cunning ways of getting away with things. This is not speaking up your heart and mind, but deceiving yourself. The third group are the 'escapists' and 'global peace lovers'. They 'live and let live' although things around them are incorrect. None of them are right in the way they approach difficult conversations.

Either you are a nice person avoiding a difficult conversation or you are the one who shares a very good relationship with the person giving the message. Apart from these, you keep quiet in certain time and in some others you want to respond back. While it makes sense to hold back at times, it is definitely not right to 'hold yourself back' forever. People will take you for granted.

The other reasons that also hold us back from having a difficult conversation are our past bitter experiences, a mechanism to self-defence, unconscious anxiety of handling the conversation poorly, appearing foolish, being disliked, fear, cultural background and values, being looked down in the organisation where you are working, lack of time and we believe things would just be right one day. For example, 'He is about to retire', or 'We cannot afford to lose him' or 'Things could get worse than this'. Our inability to come out of the comfort zone also holds us back. We love talking in a 'neutral' environment where things will rarely go wrong. Accustomed to this practice we find it difficult to readjust in difficult environments.

A survey by Bravely says it all. Seventy per cent of employees are avoiding difficult conversations with their boss, colleagues or direct reportees and 53 per cent of employees are handling 'toxic situations' just by ignoring them.[2]

THERE IS NO 'ESCAPE': WE MUST TALK

The more we delay, the more the issue escalates. It impacts our career, lives, both personal and professional, and our business to a tremendous extent.

Difficult conversations could be of different types. The first is when you have to say a 'no'. You are getting overburdened with your work and still to make the other person feel happy, you say a 'yes'. Although

---

[2] https://learn.workbravely.com/hubfs/Understanding-the-Conversation-Gap.pdf?t =1533596048056&utm_campaign=smart%20brief%20test&utm_source=hs_ automation&utm_medium=email&utm_content=64321921&_hsenc=p2ANqtz-_4k_ KzRnQICrerxB5GrOXEMMWshILmigMT3ElhTx6htsOUK3kcp7H-J_GAqZMvlAdILhbkk DX2sEDVSXIQdx9e-xqh8A&_hsmi=64321921 (accessed on 22 May 2019).

we desire to say the opposite, our mouth says something different. Simple things like coming to office on a weekend, stretching beyond what is normal course of business and many more.

Walia was the branch head of a bank. Responsible for the loans portfolio, he used to make his sales team come on weekends (both the days). Just because the main guy was coming to office, his managers came and so did his sales team, although productivity used to be near zero on a weekend.

The second is when you have to handle rude and 'toxic' people and their behaviour. For example, your manager shouts at you in front of the whole team sitting just beside you because you did not achieve your targets.

Rita was leading a team. A new joinee was given to her for a particular sales area. Every day in the morning when the team call happened, Rita used to religiously shout at this new executive. The poor guy used to sit quietly and listen to her. The entire team started asking this guy, 'Why do not you speak up?'

The third are the sensitive situations which require you to talk with people. Such as the case of death of your colleagues which you need to convey or poor washroom usage etiquette of your staff.

The sales team of a company was called for a meeting. The women were excluded from this meeting. The sales manager started explaining about the usage of the toilet and reminded everyone that it is a shared facility.

The fourth is when you have to deliver bad news. Firing an employee, bad performance of an employee, putting the promotion of an employee on hold and so on.

You are getting promoted. One of your best friends and colleagues were also in the run to getting promoted. But you won the race. You will now need to convey this message to your friends.

Avoiding all these puts you at a greater risk. A study done in USA showed that employees spend about 2.8 hours per week dealing with different kinds of conflict, which translates into $359 billion in paid hours.[3]

The biggest risk is losing your reputation. The next biggest risk is spoiling a relationship. Along with this productivity will fall, your self-esteem will take a hit and people will consider you as a weak leader. You will be making your team members dysfunctional and negatively impact their performance. Avoidance will also lead to bad mouthing, criticisms and gossips.

A family-owned business with three partners was doing great. The business was started by their parents and had been kept closely tied up within the family members. The business had been running successfully for over 75 years. Many of the employees were now second generation employees. However, they reached a stage when things were very comfortable and they did not know what next to do. They hired an external consultant whose job was to suggest them a way forward. The consultant observed that the senior members rarely spoke anything against the founders and it was not that they would be penalized for it, but did it to preserve the cultural background of the organization. This had eventually percolated amongst the entire team who found it extremely tough to talk with these founders though they were easily accessible. So the consultants in one of the meetings asked the founder to leave the room and opened it up for discussions. After some inhibition, all opened up. However, immediately after the partners were called back in the room, they stopped speaking. The consultant realized that the root cause is the employees and the higher ups do not talk unpleasant things with their founders.

DO NOT CONTEMPLATE: FIRST ASK YOURSELF THE RIGHT QUESTIONS

> Let us make a special effort to stop communicating with each other, so we can have some conversation.
>
> —Mark Twain

---

[3] https://www.themyersbriggs.com/download/item/f39a8b7fb4fe4daface552d9f485c825 (accessed on 23 May 2019).

Musk is a fragrance found in the navel of the musk deer. This odour comes from the navel of the deer. The deer gets excited at the attractive odour and searches for it everywhere, but is unable to find it. Finally, the deer grows angry and restless, and jumps from the high cliffs plunging to death.[4]

This is what happens to us because we do not know the source of the problem. When confronted or when we want to start a difficult conversation, there are so many things that our minds prompt us to say, but we are unable to pin the real issue or the naval of the deer from where the fragrance or the problem is coming from. While some of the problems are easy, like a poor performance, some are not, like a sales guy with stellar performance but haphazard, unplanned and unwilling to listen.

We make assumptions because we imagine and we are quick to judge people. Our minds weave what we allow them to. These thoughts are mostly on the wrong side of the fence.

Leena reports to you and you are running short of time on a particular day. You want some work to be done quickly. You tell yourself, 'If I give it to Leena, that will be the end. She will definitely be saying a no or delaying it.' What you have done is that you have allowed your mind to wonder and weave things about Leena which may be factually incorrect. You are not focusing on the problem, but on the possible outcomes. Instead, if you ask her, she probably might complete it without saying a no or may not be delaying it. In case you are sure she would delay the task, ask the right questions, 'Why is Leena doing that?' or 'Why will she not be able to submit the reports?

The second set of right questions that you should be asking is: 'Does this impact me or the business?' or 'Is this having a significant impact on my people'? If it does, it is time to take the elephant out of the room and discuss, but not before you have ensured certain checks are in place.

---

[4] https://www.expandinglight.org/blog/meditation/meditation-teacher-training/ happiness-is-within-the-himalayan-musk-deer/ (accessed on 23 May 2019).

While this method holds true for handling rude and toxic people, their behaviour and the people who frequent you with a 'no', this does not hold true/holds partially true for the third and the fourth category of difficult conversations—when you are dealing with sensitive situations or delivering a bad news. While you may or may not be measuring the impact, however you will need to ask a 'how'. How do I tell this to the people?

HAVE YOU DONE THE SANITY CHECK?

A travelogue published by Mark Twain in 1897, *Following the Equator: A Journey around the World* had this famous quote: 'Truth is stranger than fiction, but it is because fiction is obliged to stick to possibilities; Truth isn't.' Before you embark on taking up difficult conversations, you need to put some checks in place. The first is to ask, 'What has happened?' Inquire within yourself. In this you try to differentiate between what you feel versus what actually is and what your pre-conceived notions are. There is a difference between what you feel vis-à-vis what actually happened. The 'data' or the information you have is important for the conversation. Do not allow your assumptions to come in between. Second keep your emotions in check and keep your mind open. An open mind acts wonderfully well. Keeping your mind open and emotions in check will allow you to accept or listen to others. Remember that you are not saying a 'no'. You are providing an alternate path. Third find out the source of the problem. Even if this takes time, spend some of your efforts in identifying the root cause. A lot of disagreement is because both the parties are not updated about the right set of information. Assumptions and feelings are a reason for disagreements. Hearing things from people and believing them to be true is the worst of all and the primary reason for disagreements.

The next step is to set an objective for the difficult conversation. How do you want to end the conversation? Do you want to maintain the relationship after the conversation, just inform, tell the person how bad you felt or do you want the other person to make some changes to his behaviour? In some cases the objective could be like knocking your head against a wall, like changing the behaviour. If you encounter such situations, try for a couple of times before you give up on it. You may also try alternatives, such as asking him to meet a coach or give him training which would help. Sometimes even the best of the plans backfire. People whom you are talking to start shouting, crying and threaten to report. You suddenly feel clueless on 'what's next'. Keeping or thinking of an alternate course of action is also important. You may just decide to conclude a discussion or be silent and wait to hear out the other person or try to adopt an alternate path of redressal without harming the person in any ways. In some cases, just allowing it to 'let go' also makes sense. At least you tried.

Should we or should we not start with a difficult conversation? Unfortunately, there are no checklists for it nor a definite answer.

THE DON'TS OF A DIFFICULT CONVERSATION

A conversation is a dialogue, not a monologue. That's why there are so few good conversations: due to scarcity, two intelligent talkers seldom meet.

—Truman Capote

When you start the conversation, there are a few things that you must keep in mind. First it is important to listen as much as speak. You should double your ability to listen than to speak. Remember to give the other person a good empathetic hearing. Ask questions and rephrase. Keep the discussion on track. Remember that it is a conversation. Second be confident of what you say. You have all the information with you and you are clear with what you want to say. Therefore, display confidence in what you say as well as in your body language. Do not get defensive like, 'Oh…It was not my fault. It just happened.' Third come straight to the point. Start with, 'I would like to tell you that….' Do not beat around the bush. Be direct, yet very specific. Fourth do not throw your weight around; mind what and how you say. Just because someone reports to you and you have the authority, avoid using them. Be careful with your words. Using indecent language and swearing or cursing words could be extremely detrimental. Avoid jumping to a conclusion or judging the person.

Some other don'ts of difficult conversations are interrupting while talking, multitasking while talking, pointing your fingers, calling out names, yelling, crying and being rude. Avoid leaving the conversation without an agreement. Find out a common solution. Difficult conversations are really not difficult. They are just like other conversations; the problem comes only after we 'label' them as difficult ones. Talk as if it is just another conversation. Never script it down.

WORDS TO AVOID IN A DIFFICULT CONVERSATION

> Words are singularly the most powerful force available to humanity. We can choose to use this force constructively with words of encouragement, or destructively using words of despair. Words have energy and power with the ability to help, to heal, to hinder, to hurt, to harm, to humiliate and to humble.
>
> —Yehuda Berg

Words are powerful and what we say is equally important to how we say it. We use words, knowingly or unknowingly, in a context which could mean altogether different, later to apologize. 'I am sorry, but I really did not mean to hurt you.' The problem often lies with the meaning of the words and how we say them. While different usages and contexts to words could be infinite, here are some of them for you to consider.

'I think this is a bad idea to merge the two units together.' Instead of that you could say, 'I think we should look at all the possibilities before merging the two units together. We need to be careful before we start doing that.' While giving bad news to people, like firing a vendor, you can say, 'You have not been supplying us what we want and there has been uninformed delays. We are therefore cancelling your contract.' An alternative way to say this is, 'Two areas which you require to improve are maintaining the delivery schedules and delivering the right products. Unless you improve on these parameters, we will not be able to take your services.' During the course of your conversation, saying, 'My immediate priority is to close the reports. That is what my boss has asked me to do' sounds much better than 'I will not be doing this. That is not why I have been hired for.'

We often say, 'I know that.' Instead, a better thing to say it is, 'Why do you feel so? Can you please explain?'

Some words can bring the conversations to a dead end. They kill difficult conversations, such as 'wow', 'that's cool' and 'interesting'. Conversations also get killed with certain words, like, 'Mac, the targets you have set to deliver in this quarter are very difficult.' The response comes back as, 'Let's see'. This is a conversation killer. Instead, it is better to respond as, 'I know they are difficult, but we will work out to make this achievable.'

Avoid the usage of 'weasel words'. These are used when someone wants to actually give a clear answer or seem like they've given a clear answer, but have said something vague. For example, using 'often', 'some', 'many', 'possibly'. Others such as 'Many people say', 'It is claimed', 'We are told', 'People often believe' weaken the difficult conversations.

Avoid the usage of 'you'. For example, 'You are the team leader and it is your responsibility to inform me about the warning signs of this project.' Instead you can say, 'Being the team leader, a little proactiviness in warning me would have helped in avoiding this.' Another example of this would be, 'You don't know your stuff.' A good way to rephrase this is, 'I am unable to understand this.' Remember, 'I' is safer than 'you' in difficult conversations.

Use 'and' more than 'but'. The latter is associated with a negative feeling. For example, 'I know you all have put in lot of hard work, but....' However, the 'and' stance makes it sound more pleasant. 'I know that you all have put in a lot of hard work for the last couple of weeks and you had to stretch yourself beyond the normal working hours....'

Keep your negative vocabulary in check. At least while using it, make it a little more pleasant to the ears. For example, 'I knew you will not be able to do this work' or 'Nothing is more important to you than making the lives of others miserable.' Instead of this, a better way to say it is, 'Being a little prompt would have helped you close this work in time' or 'A better professional approach is expected from the employees which results into better team bonding.'

YOUR MESSAGE

There is no conversation more boring than the one where everybody agrees.

—Michel de Montaigne

Situation 1

Boss: I am sorry, but I could not get you a promotion in this cycle.

Employee: But why? I have exceeded in all the parameters that you had put for me.

Boss: As a company, we have not done fairly well and the organization has put a hold on all the promotions for this year. Even if there is news of a couple of promotions, they are a few.

Employee: If that is the case, then I will have to look for other opportunities. The employee walks out of the room.

Situation 2

Boss: I am sorry, but I could not get you a promotion in this cycle.

Employee: But why? I have exceeded in all the parameters that you had put for me.

Boss: As a company, we have not done fairly well and the organization has put a hold on all the promotions for this year. Even if there is news of a couple of promotions, they are a few.

Employee: Well, in that case, I want to know how I have been doing and what is needed for me to grow. I am also looking into my growth perspective. I understand it is a bad time for the company and you would have really tried hard to get me a promotion.

(Boss provides his feedback and suggestion.)

Employee: Is there anything else that you would want me to do?

(Boss suggests some more)

Employee: In that case, let me give it a try for one more time and I will be checking with you on how I have fared and if I am right on track for the next round of promotions.

The employee is having a difficult conversation with his manager, unhappy about not getting promoted. The boss cannot do anything much in such a situation. The first situation comes to a dead-end because the employee does not want the discussion to be taken forward. In the second situation, it is more acceptable and agreeable to both the parties. The end result is more positive than the first one.

Difficult conversation is not going to be easy. The person listening to your message could have a range of emotions. If we were to be in the same position, we would have probably behaved in the same way, ideally. For example, you have to fire a reportee and you are talking to him about this. Getting hurt, embarrassed, tears, shouting, threatening or in the best case willing to change could be some of the emotions displayed. Before you start, be ready for these outcomes. It would be good if the person in front accepts them. However, you may also be at the receiving end of these emotions. Prepare yourself well.

The second aspect of difficult conversations is the right timing. You just do not call anyone at any time to start the conversation. You need to prepare mentally before the conversation. Also you need to inform the person that you are going to have a conversation. So ask before you set up conversations. A good way to do this is, 'Can we meet for some time today in the afternoon. I need to talk about or give a feedback on....' Ensure you don't delay these conversations. Have them as quickly as possible. Choose a closed-door room for discussions. If you need to involve someone, please invite the right person to accompany you. For example, a disciplinary issue with an employee may need you to involve the HR.

Your messages in difficult conversations must have a good beginning. You can possibly start the conversations with a good strong supportive statement. Ensure that you are not stretching yourself too long. For example, a right beginning would be: 'I'd like to talk about...' or 'I think we have different perspective about....'

When you are delivering difficult conversations, check on to three points. First n*ever delay the conversations.* Do not say things after a lot of time has passed, when the conversation really does not matter. Second is to be ready with the facts, and sieve your perceptions and feelings from the facts. The third is to be brief and clear with these messages. Beating around the bush and taking time to start the message do not help. There is no need to exchange pleasantries before you start your difficult conversations.

The first, of course, is not to delay the conversations. Never push the conversations, as we have discussed earlier, because that has a tremendous impact in the near future.

Second is *state the facts.* Differentiate between what you feel versus the truth. You are introspecting and analysing yourself here. This could be difficult, but not impossible. For example, 'I reached the venue ten minutes late' rather than, 'I reached the venue late.' The first one is more clear a message than the second one. Few other examples of facts would be: 'Seema always comes up with an excuse of not doing a work.' Instead a better thing would be: 'Seema has not completed the last three tasks that was given to her.'

While you are stating your facts, ensure that you are not being *judgmental.* For example, 'It is absolutely inappropriate of you to come late to the meetings.' We made mistakes on two accounts. First in using a 'you' and second by being judgmental. The alternative to this would be, 'It is expected that all of us come to meetings on time' or 'I want everyone to be present in the meetings so that we all can make it fruitful.'

Avoid blaming people. 'The reason why we have failed to get this done is because of your pathetic attitude.' This is easy to do, especially when you have the power. Also you are not stating the fact and have made a cocktail of your emotions and judgements. Instead, a better way of saying this is, 'How can we do this better the next time?'

Never *exaggerate*. For example, 'I have told you this a hundred times and it seems it does get into your head' or 'Nothing seems more important to you than your personal career ambitions.' Instead of saying these, the better way to say is: 'I need you to focus more on the work that you are doing' or 'As a part of this organization, you need to keep the organizational perspectives in mind, balancing them with your personal ambitions.'

The third point is to be *brief* and *clear* with the messages. When you present your message, avoid providing too much of explanations and keep it to the minimum possible words. For example, 'I think Sameer, you need to focus on your work because since the last year I have been observing you. I find that your quality of work has been severely impacted and you are unable to perform well. This is affecting the team morale and I hope that you do a little better.' In this message you have already violated many of the rules of a difficult conversation. To keep it simple and easy, an alternate is: 'Sameer, I want you to focus on the quality of your deliverables.'

While delivering a difficult conversation, maintain a positive body language. A smile on the face, sitting erect and upright without crossing legs or hands, focusing on our tone of voice, which should not be too low or high and maintaining an eye contact with whom we are speaking with. Nod your heads and smile affirming to what has been said. Keep a tab on the other person's body language too. This will give you a feel of what how the person is receiving the message.

Difficult conversations rarely go as scheduled and while it is important to appreciate the perspective of the other, the goal however is the one you started with. Keep a check on how the discussion has been going, slow down if necessary and revisit the discussion mentally. Always keep the context in mind, the reason why you had started the discussion. While other issues may crop up during the discussion, park it for some time and take them up at a different time.

Closing the discussion is another important aspect. You must try and do three things. First build a consensus and then a commitment. For example, 'We are agreeing to…' or 'We are not agreeing to….' Once this has been done, build a commitment. For example, 'We will therefore…' or 'What do you think should be the next step?' Second follow up on what you have said. If you had given some a feedback and that person has been working to improve on it, do not forget to appreciate and mention the changes he has brought in. Third bring the conversation to a logical end. Here are some of the ways to do it: 'I have made my point very clear. These are my expectations' or 'Just to clarify, this is what we have spoken till now' or 'Let us review this after a couple of days. I will set up a meeting soon.' Now the action that you want the other person to take is the one which you should be closing with. Ensure that you close with a touch of respect, genuineness and sincerity.

CONCLUSION

> Never talk for half a minute without pausing and giving others a
> chance to join in.
>
> —Sydney Smith

The outcome of a difficult conversation is a bitter pill that one needs to swallow and no matter how much you try, it might turn out to be different from what you had expected. This chapter therefore presents you some guidelines that you should follow for conversations that are difficult. These guidelines will help you steer the conversation in the best possible manner. Remember that the outcome you had been anticipating from the discussion will take its own time. The person whom you have been talking to will take some time to review and reflect before he starts making the change. It is a time-consuming process. Never rush the person through and do not forget to appreciate when he has really made the efforts to make the change.

8 The Art of Presenting

WHAT PRESENTATIONS ARE ALL ABOUT?

There are only two types of speakers in the world. 1. The nervous and 2. Liars.

— Mark Twain

Glossophobia is the fear of public speaking, and like it or not we all have it. Research shows that it is common and affects up to 75 per cent of the total population.[1] Presenting in itself is no easy task and it requires a lot of guts and courage to go up, stand and talk in front of an audience. Mahatma Gandhi, Warren Buffett, Abraham Lincoln and Thomas Jefferson have one thing in common. All of them dreaded public speaking. All these great leaders overcame this fear to become great and wonderful speakers whose speeches and talks are still revered and worth reflecting upon.[2] This is the first biggest challenge of presenting and it is about 'you' and conquering your personal fears. Presentations therefore cannot be done in an environment of personal fear. You must overcome it.

---

[1] Rosemary Black, 'Glossophobia (Fear of Public Speaking): Are You Glossophobic?' *Psycom*, 2019. https://www.psycom.net/glossophobia-fear-of-public-speaking (accessed on 27 May 2019).

[2] Nayomi Chibana, 'Amazing Leaders Who Once Had Stage Fright and How They Overcame It,' *Visme*, 2019. https://visme.co/blog/amazing-leaders-who-once-had-crippling-stage-fright-and-how-they-overcame-it/ (accessed on 27 May 2019).

Presentation is about connecting with your audience. It is about taking your ideas and thoughts to the people who are listening to you. You are connecting with them, trying to persuade them or motivate them to act and in some cases you are trying to inform them. So how do you connect with your audience? While some advice to knit a story, some others try to bridge the gap between what the audience knows and where you want to take them. Create a story that your audience will believe in. It is like using Google Maps to go from Point A to Point B with multiple paths.

SpaceX founder and billionaire Elon Musk wanted to launch a program for people to travel to Mars with hopes of saving humanity. He said, 'What I really want to do here is make Mars seem possible' and in his 90-minute slideshow he tried to convince a bunch of astrophysicists about its possibility. Using his unorthodox presentation style and capturing the imagination of the people he delivered his ideas.[3]

The audience is not interested in knowing about the tons of data that you have put in your presentation or the bullets that you want them to remember. They in fact will not remember the message that you want them to remember. The success or failure will be measured by the impact it had on each one of the individuals sitting and listening to you. A demonstration or a display, an experiment, presentation of the prototype, a try-it-yourself does it all. It gives the audience a reason to believe in your ideas and thoughts. Your objective therefore is to become audience centric. Use different methodologies to prove your point and guide them through for them to understand and act.

An Inconvenient Truth was a documentary film made in 2006 by Davis Guggenheim about former USA's Vice President Al Gore's

---

[3] Lenny DeFranco, 'The 8 Most Influential PowerPoint Presentations In History,' The Abacus Blog, 13 November 2017, https://blog.abacus.com/8-influential-powerpoint-presentations/ (accessed on 27 May 2019).

campaign to educate people about global warming. The Vice President used a slide show to present to the world his idea of global warming. Producer Laurie David saw this presentation and with Lawrence Bender converted it into a film. The documentary won two Academy Awards for Best Documentary Feature and Best Original Song and became the eleventh highest grossing documentary film to date in USA.

Steve Jobs was a master in delivering his presentations. He got it right every time and he would create a wonderful experience in the new products he launched. The audience connects with you only when you deliver a wonderful experience for them. The launch of iPod (2001) was a unique experience.

He asked the audience, 'Why music?' Then he went on answer, 'We love music. And it's always good to do something you love. More importantly, music is a part of everyone's life. Music has been around forever. It's always good to do something you love. More importantly, music's a part of everyone's life. Everyone. Music's been around forever. It will always be around. This is not a speculative market. And, because it's a part of everyone's life, it's a very large target market. All around the world. It knows no boundaries.'

Steve Jobs then demonstrated why an iPod would make a tremendous difference to the existing business.

Be clear on your message and what experience you want to deliver. Have you showed them sufficient credible data to drive your point and something different for them to experience? Have you presented your data in a mundane and boring slide deck or in an easily digestible byte?

The last, of course, is your style, how you talk, your non-verbal communication, your practice and rehearsing what you have done. This will add wholesomeness to your presentation. How you communicate, how you start and what you say have a great impact on your audience.

Dr Jill Bolte Taylor, presented a TED Talk, 'Stroke of Insight' which is one of the most popular TED Talks, and has been viewed over a million times on the Internet.[4]

TED speaker, Chris Anderson mentions in one of his talks, 'You use the power of language to weave together concepts that already exist in your listeners' minds—but not your language, their language. You start where they are. The speakers often forget that many of the terms and concepts they live with are completely unfamiliar to their audiences.'[5]

Your voice and body language must communicate authority of the topic that you are speaking about, display confidence about what you are saying and energy to energize your audience.

KNOWING THE BARE MINIMUM

There are always three speeches, for every one you actually gave. The one you practiced, the one you gave, and the one you wish you gave.

—Dale Carnegie

The bare minimum that you must know to get your presentation right are: first, who is your audience, second, where are you presenting and third, the theme of the presentation.

Your preparation is the key to success. 'Ninety per cent of how well the talk will go is determined before the speaker steps on the platform' (Somers White). If you have not prepared well, the audience will

---

[4] Inc.com, '5 Key Steps to Rehearsing a Presentation Like the Best TED Speakers,' *Inc. com*, 30 July 2018, https://www.inc.com/carmine-gallo/5-key-steps-to-rehearsing-a-presentation-like-best-ted-speakers.html (accessed on 27 May 2019).

[5] Chris Anderson, 'TED's Secret to Great Public Speaking,' *TED Studio*, 2019. https://www.ted.com/talks/chris_anderson_teds_secret_to_great_public_speaking/transcript?referrer=playlist-how_to_make_a_great_presentation (accessed on 27 May 2019).

come to know and you will not be able to hold their attention span. Poor preparation reduces your credibility. You should therefore start working on the first factor: understanding the audience. It can't get worst if you do not know who the audience is. Speaking to a group of senior executives would be different from the way you address new joinees in the organization. The level of knowledge of the audience will also tell you where you begin and end. Remember not to generalize. The demographics is also a critical component. It becomes easier for you to connect. You can tell them things that they can relate to. If you know the audience or at least few of them, you can piggyback on them if you want to. Understanding the audience expectation or keeping a tab of what the audience expects is important. This is also a critical component of understanding the audience. The last aspect of understanding the audience is the possible outcome. Are you going to see any hostility or indifference or a neutral stand in behaviour after the audience has heard you? Few other questions that will help you know more about them are: What do they wish to achieve at the end of the talk, what do they think, what is happening in their company and business. Know your audience as much as you can and to as much depth as possible. This will give you a feeling of what you need to say, how you need to plan and how you need to pitch.

Akash was invited to a large gathering of senior executives of a multinational company. The company had just fired about 500 senior level executives and they were worried about, who would be next? Akash was asked to talk about 'leadership and communication for senior executives' with the audience. As it happens, there were further rumours of layoffs on the day Akash was slated for his presentation. While Akash presented, no one bothered to listen, all were checking their mobile devices if anything worse had come.

After a presentation that I had done, some of the participants stayed in touch. During a conversation later, I asked them, 'So did you get a chance to implement, some of the ideas I suggested?' Someone replied, 'Our company has not paid us for the last six months. Do you think, we have the necessary motivation to implement, what you had suggested?'

Audience expectation is the most underrated aspect of presenting. Often the organizers as well as the presenters take this for granted. The presenters do not ask the right questions and the organizers do not answer them with enthusiasm, creating a recipe for failure.

The venue is the second most important aspect of presenting. You should know what is available and what is not. While you are planning for your presentation, keep the challenges of the location in mind. Some factors such as the size of the room or the number of people attending may not be right for having a workshop or a discussion. Some presentations, which require in depth discussions, for example, need to be done with smaller groups. Sometimes you may be sending your slide deck only to realize that the room does not have a LCD projector or your device is incompatible with the hardware they are using. You will find that many presentations get stuck because of incompatibility of devices. If you can, visit the venue to check the entry and exit points especially as you may tend to get disturbed while presenting if you see a set of people moving in and out every time.

The third is the theme of the presentation. Are you talking to your audience in an informal or a formal setting and what do you aim to convey? Is it only information that you are presenting or are you persuading the audience. You also need to know the time that is allotted for the presentation. When someone else is organizing the conference ask these three questions: first, how much time has been allotted to me. Second, what do you want me to speak about and the objective to be achieved, and third, where is the venue and does it have all the necessary arrangements.

Shraddha came to Usman and asked him, 'Can you please do this session for us?' Usman said, 'Yes I will be doing it.' Shraddha said, 'But Usman I cannot give you the allotted two hours for the session. A board member is coming to address another group of employees at the same venue; I can give you only one hour to do this. Is it okay for you?' Usman said, 'Does not matter, tell me the time and I will tailor it.' Usman also calculated mentally. Since he would be presenting in the same venue where the director was coming to address, he would get another 15 minutes less because the employees who were supposed to meet the director for the next meeting would start turning up. So he would have to wrap it up in 45 minutes.

I was invited for a talk in one of the B-schools. I had enquired it all. I asked them to download some of the videos for the session and keep it ready. A day before I checked with my point of contact and the faculty confirmed that it had been done. I reached the venue and during my presentation when I asked for the videos the student responsible for it said that he could not download them as the Internet had not been working for a couple of days. They were apologetic but it was too late.

PLANNING AND WRITING THE PRESENTATION

> People will forget what you said, people will forget what you did, but people will never forget how you made them feel.
>
> —Maya Angelou

The CEO of a MNC firm was the diamond sponsor to a prestigious event. He was invited as a speaker to a conference which would be attended by leaders from across the globe. He had to make his mark. He identified a group of professional who could generate ideas, build a narrative, slide decks, allied material and groom him to deliver the talk.

In the final stages of the rehearsal the CEO said, 'I am finding it very difficult to say what I have been told to. It feels like I am a parrot. My feelings, words everything is doctored. This is not my usual self and I find this very uncomfortable. This is not my style.'

One of his team members asked him, 'So how do you want to say this?'

The CEO gave a small demonstration of what he wanted to say. The team member said, 'That's it…Just stick to that. Forget what they are saying and be yourself.'

When you say things that are doctored, you rarely speak with confidence. If you want to deliver something which touches the mind and the heart of the audience, never try to build a script. Never ever write down a presentation. Draw a sketch of what you want to do and how you want to go ahead.

The first step, therefore, for a great start is to brainstorm. Do this with a couple of people who are experts and get as many ideas as possible. You can also jot down the points on a notepad or folder whenever you remember them. While you will be getting many ideas, try to keep them together. Ensure that you think about it from multiple perspectives. The ideas will not be in an order, but they will guide you to the final pitch.

The next step is to group these ideas logically. Use a mind map to do that. Group the ideas generated into branches with sub-themes and place your ideas to each of the branches. You will get a holistic picture. Once you have done, keep the ones which matter. You can also follow an alternate approach. Have a few central thoughts. Then write down how you will drive this down with examples. You may use stories, videos, demos, examples and so on.

It is now time to put it together. Remember the cardinal rule: *'Tell 'em what you're gonna tell 'em, tell 'em and then tell 'em what you've told 'em.'* Keep it neat with a clear flow. Keep asking yourself are you being able to transition the audience from idea to another without any point-less examples? First prepare the main body of the speech. Keep the beginning and the end for the last. Never write word to word. You may however write down some key phrases which you want to reiterate to make the presentation powerful.

No idea is worth a million words. If you are able to express your ideas and thoughts, and convince on a 'cocktail napkin' that is the best idea. That is your central idea.

Two men, Rollin King and Herb Kelleher walked into a bar. They ordered for their drinks and one of them drew a triangle on a cocktail napkin. At the top was Dallas, bottom left was San Antonio and the bottom right had Houston and said, 'This is the business plan. Fly between them as many times as you can every day, so that flying becomes an alternative to travelling by road.' This is how Southwest Airlines began—on a cocktail napkin.[6]

The best ideas sometimes come from sketches on the back of a beer mat. One such idea was the Virgin Blue. The sketches on the beer mats were done by Brett Godfrey, who was the CFO for Virgin Express. On a phone call between Brett and Richard Branson, the former found his notes written on the back of a beer mat.[7]

THE BEGINNING AND THE END

It usually takes me more than three weeks to prepare a good impromptu speech.

—Mark Twain

The attention span of your audience decreases with time and you should keep this in mind. Keep your presentations crisp and short, and figure out a way to engage the audience. The audience starts on an attention peak and as you progress, it troughs down and starts rising up towards the end. Engagement with the audience and holding up their interest is the key. David Ogilvy, built one of the largest advertising agencies in the world and he summarized the start of any commercial with his famous one-liner, 'When you advertise fire-extinguishers, open with the fire.'[8]

If there is someone introducing you, ensure that you give your brief in a way that the audience feels curious to know more from

[6] W. F. Strong, 'The Airline That Started with a Cocktail Napkin', *Texas Standard*, 20 April 2016, https://www.texasstandard.org/stories/the-airline-that-started-with-a-cocktail-napkin/ (accessed on 28 May 2019).

[7] Richard Branson, 'Sometimes the Best Ideas Come on the Back of a Beer Mat,' *Virgin*, 14 November 2017, https://www.virgin.com/richard-branson/sometimes-best-ideas-come-back-beer-mat (accessed on 28 May 2019).

[8] Dean Rieck, 'Direct Creative, The Wit and Wisdom of David Ogilvy,' Direct Creative, 2019. http://www.directcreative.com/the-wit-and-wisdom-of-david-ogilvy.html (accessed on 28 May 2019).

you like, 'Our speaker for today has over 25 years of experience in six industry verticals. He has transformed organizations and lead global teams. Please join your hand together for....' If you have a longer introduction, focus on building expectancy and your credibility. The lamest way to do so is saying, 'I am Hory Sankar and I'm happy to be here.'

It is now time for you to begin. There are various ways to begin, however demonstrate confidence. You can start by *complimenting* the audience, for example, 'I am talking to a group of people working in an organization who cares about others and the environment, and is the best in business'; or a *positive* statement like, 'It is wonderful meeting a bunch of young and wonderful people like you who have set out to start off on their own'; or a statement that will *provoke thoughts or curiosity* like, 'If I were to tell you that you will live up to 85 years, how many of you have planned for such a long life after retirement?'; or a *historical fact* or a *shocking incident* like, '50 per cent of the people sitting in this room will not be ending their career from where they are starting'; or a with a *quote, humour, question, poll* or *starting with a story* or *by interacting with one another or a small ice-breaker.* There are many ways to do it, however, choose the way that fits the best, you are comfortable with and what the audience can relate to.

Close with a memory that will last.

Winston Churchill, ended a speech with the note, 'Never was so much owed by so many to so few' about the Air Force pilots who were fighting the Battle of Britain against the German Luftwaffe (1940).[9]

Restate and summarize what you have said, actions you need to take and benefits the audience would derive. For example, 'We have discussed...and the main points were....' You can ask your *audience to action.* For example, 'With bright people sitting in this audience, it

---

[9] Wikipedia, 'Never Was So Much Owed by So Many to So Few,' *Wikipedia,* https://en.wikipedia.org/wiki/Never_was_so_much_owed_by_so_many_to_so_few (accessed on 28 May 2019).

would not take efforts to weave a success story. We will make the next two years the best in the history of this institution.' You can close the presentation with *a story or a comic strip, or humour*, however ensure that it fits very well into the scheme of your presentation.

For example, when I talk to students, about the use of data and statistics, I tell them this humorous story:

A statistics professor had taken one of his students for hunting. When he saw a bird sitting on the branch of a tree, he pointed his gun at it and fired. The bullet missed the bird to its right by an inch. He fired a second bullet. It missed the bird to its left by an inch. After this the bird flew away.

The statistics professor now looked at his student and said, 'Don't get disappointed. On an 'average', we have killed the bird.'

While the laugh subsides, I tell them, 'Interpret data with care'.

You can also close by *inspiring them* or by asking a *rhetoric question* like, the

Jimmy Carter–Ronald Reagan presidential debate: Ronald Reagan asked the audience a question: 'Are you any better off now than you were four years ago?' That question summarized what President Carter did not do.[10]

REHEARSE YOUR SPEECH

Always give a speech that you would like to hear.

—Andrii Sedniev

Professor Anders Ericsson wrote a research paper in 1993, titled, 'The Role of Deliberate Practice in the Acquisition of Expert Performance',

---

[10] Robert Rackleff, '6 Memorable Ways to Close a Speech,' Ragan, 7 November 2011, https://www.ragan.com/6-memorable-ways-to-close-a-speech-2/ (accessed on 28 May 2019).

which was later used by Malcolm Gladwell in his book, *Outliers*. The research pointed out a simple fact. If you want to be an expert, put in about 10,000 hours of practice. Performers, therefore, put in hours of practice trying to improve. However, they are clear on what they want to change, ask for feedback and work towards improving themselves.[11]

For example, take the Lincoln's Gettysburg Address. The Address is memorized by people today as perhaps one of the best pieces of oratory. Many people had opined that it was written on the back of an envelope when Lincoln was travelling by train to Gettysburg. This was not the truth. Lincoln spent almost two weeks on the speech. As president he often turned down opportunities to speak as he thought that he was a poor impromptu speaker. Similar was the case with Martin Luther King's, 'I have a dream' speech.[12]

According to Carmine Gallo, 'Winston Churchill, Prime Minister of UK, is considered as one of the greatest orators. However, as people put it, that he had almost frozen, in one of his earlier speeches he gave to the House of Commons, as a newly elected representative. He spend years practicing, building mastery over his oratory skills, getting obsessed with his choice of words and substituting with short impact words. Steve Jobs was also a novice when he started off, practicing off to become a master in how he presented.'[13]

The key to success, therefore, lies in rehearsing and practice. The more the better. The first step to do is to start off with notes. Make a

[11] Shana Lebowitz, 'A Top Psychologist Says There's Only One Way To Become the Best in Your Field—But Not Everyone Agrees,' *Business Insider*, 12 June 2016, https://www.businessinsider.in/A-top-psychologist-says-theres-only-one-way-to-become-the-best-in-your-field-but-not-everyone-agrees/articleshow/52715262.cms (accessed on 28 May 2019).

[12] Ken Jennings, 'The Debunker: Did Lincoln Write the Gettysburg Address on an Envelope?' *Woot*, https://www.woot.com/blog/post/the-debunker-did-lincoln-write-the-emancipation-proclamation-on-an-envelope (accessed on 28 May 2019).

[13] Carmine Gallo, 'Steve Jobs and Winston Churchill Didn't Start Out As Great Speakers,' *Forbes*, 25 November 2014, https://www.forbes.com/sites/carminegallo/2014/11/25/steve-jobs-and-winston-churchill-didnt-start-out-as-great-speakers/#1904713296a2 (accessed on 28 May 2019).

note of what you want to say in each of the slides. Ensure that you time your presentation. Once you are comfortable doing that alone, present it to a smaller audience. While you present to the audience, ask for feedback. Ask for specific feedback on the quality, things that can be improved, parts of the speech they did not understand and so on. If the audience says, 'It's great', it means they are not giving you the right feedback. Another good way to do this is recording the video and going through it. Keep repeating till you have perfected your pitch.

A CEO was practicing for his speech at a global conference of industries. He had rehearsed his speech about 100 times. Every time he was interrupted by someone walking in or the phone ringing, he would start from the beginning. He spent a couple of sleepless nights just to practice the entire speech. He was allotted 15 minutes for this speech.

While you rehearse, give yourself sufficient time to do it. Time yourself while rehearsing. Ensure that you are within your time limits. As you approach the D-Day, visualize the audience is in front of you. Record the presentation and take a look. If you find your present-ation to be dumb and boring, re-start. Find out ways to make it more interesting. Keep this practice on till you are contended with yourself. However, do this as many times as you can. If you feel that you will deliver it on the fly, you are thoroughly wrong. The audience will get a half-baked feeling of what you are trying to tell them. Even if you are an expert and have mastered the art and the subject, you still need to practice. Every intellectual person on this earth can stand in front of an audience and share their path-breaking research. If that would have been the mark of success, there was no need to practice data. It happens with a lot more and requires practice.

Memorizing the entire speech is a really bad idea. Never attempt to do that. It sounds cold, without emotions and if you forget or miss out, you will not be able to come back.

STARTING TO TALK

> There are three things to aim at in public speaking: first, to get
> into your subject, then to get your subject into yourself, and
> lastly, to get your subject into the heart of your audience.

> —Alexander Gregg

Now it is time for you to start your talk. After you have stepped up
on the dais to talk, the first aspect is to focus on the speed of your
speech. When you are on the stage, *walk confidently, smiling.* Look at
the audience. Remain silent for a few seconds for the audience to
settle down and start with a strong beginning (as discussed earlier).

Focus on your *volume, pace* and *pitch.* Varying the volume of your
voice helps the audience remain tuned. If they find it difficult to hear,
you are losing their attention. If the audience is more and the room is
large, you will need to ensure that the volumes are higher. Get the
audios checked before you start talking. Speakers who are soft feel
that they are shouting at their audience, however you will need to
practice to get over this. Ensure that your words are heard across the
audience smoothly. Pitch and pace depend on what you are trying to
say and on your audience. For a board or a senior executive meeting,
a slow pitch and pace is suggested. Vary the pace of your words. Do
not go too slow or fast, which are at the extreme ends, but do not
sound monotonous as well. Remember to speak slowly then fast
because when you do that, the listeners get a chance to reflect on
what you have said. When you are fast, you will increase your pitch,
draining more energy than what is required and the impact of your
words decreases. Great speakers therefore focus on slowing down and
use the power of pauses. Display a strong energy which will exude
confidence. Ensure that you are not stumbling on the words that
you speak, filling the vacant positions of your speeches with 'ahhhs
and ummmms' (filler words) or by being too fast without pausing or
giving too many of them.

LOOK AT YOUR AUDIENCE

An ideal time to look at your audience or a person is between three to
five seconds. If you are talking to a larger group, look at the person

and run your eyes slowly from one end to another. People in the audience however have a different effect. When you look at a person, there are many people around who feel that you are actually looking at them. You therefore connect with more people. Eye contacts help you connect to your audience. Do not look at the ceilings or at the floor of the venue or at nothing or just at the papers from where you are reading your speech.

> The right word may be effective, but no word was ever as effective as a rightly timed pause.
>
> —Mark Twain

The *pauses* in your speech are very powerful. James Bond uses them perfectly. While saying his name, he says, 'Bond <PAUSE>.James Bond'. They gives you and your audiences' mind a break, allowing you to think for milliseconds and convey your words more strongly. You can also get over your filler words just by pausing. The first effective way to use this is to pause for a second or two between every two ideas. For example, 'Let us imagine that we focus more on improving the productivity for this year <PAUSE>. The impact this will have on our sales team will be…<PAUSE>.' A pause can also be used in cases when you trying to make the audience think. For example, 'The biggest challenge the technology trainers are facing is their lack of obsolescence <PAUSE>.' Why you do not tell them the reason immediately is because you are giving your audience a second or two to think. You may also pause after each idea or after every question that you have asked from the audience. Do not overdo pauses.

STAND WHILE YOU TALK

Walk around, but in a small square. Some people move from one corner of the room to another, not only distracting the audience but also exhausting themselves. Stand, but do not lean back, put your hands on your hips and cross your legs or fold your arms or put your hands in your pockets. It can make you look overconfident or underconfident. Similarly rubbing your hands, playing with your rings, changing the rings from one hand to another and playing with the change in your pockets demonstrate nervousness. Avoid them.

Words have their own significance especially on how it has been said. If you put stress on different words in your sentences, the meaning conveyed would change. When you want to emphasize, speak louder; when you want to say something off the record or sensitive, speak low. In any talk that you give, your tone and the rate of talking will vary. It will go high and low. The more variation you go through, more interesting your talk would be. Ensure that you are taking your audience through it.

Hooks connect ideas of your presentation and stitch the ideas together. You will have to smoothly transition your audience from one to another without giving them any gaps or voids. You are introduced, you open, present your first point, use a hook, present a second point, use a hook and then present the third and so on till you reach the summary or the conclusion. When you speak in a conference, use the talks delivered by others as a starting point for your talk like, 'What Mr Anand said was extremely valid.' Come early and start hearing the talks from the beginning. Connect what has been said and what you are going to say. In conferences, it is suggested that you do not start unless the protocol says so. While there are multiple ways to hook, storytelling, asking questions, interactions with the audience, ice-breakers, an exercise for the participants and games act as wonderful hooks. Transition smoothly, which can be: 'Next in my agenda is….' Complete your idea and point, and do not come back unless you really want them to connect to your earlier points.[14]

Use the power of three for your presentations, like what Abraham Lincoln did or like in William Shakespeare's *Julius Caesar*: 'government of the people, by the people and for the people' or 'veni, vidi, vici' and 'friends, Romans, countrymen.' The power of three allows you to convey your ideas clearly, highlight your key ideas and increase the retention of your audience.

Visuals as a medium of communication are powerful. We remember things which we see. There are various categories of visuals that you

---

[14] Dean Rieck, 'Direct Creative, The Wit and Wisdom of David Ogilvy,' Direct Creative, http://www.directcreative.com/the-wit-and-wisdom-of-david-ogilvy.html (accessed on 28 May 2019).

can use such as a slide deck, a whiteboard, handouts, videos, flipcharts, products, posters and more. However, there are three cardinal rules for the usage of visuals. First, do not overuse visuals. Too many of them or too colourful often kill a good presentation. Second, make it big and bold. Ensure that your visuals are big enough for the audience in the last row to look and read, effortlessly. Third, use them to make a connect with your audience to magnify the impact. Do not let the visuals hijack the presentation.

Guy Kawasaki's book *The Macintosh Way* provides its readers a section on 'How to Give Good Demo', where he suggests that good demos should be short, simple, sweet, swift and substantial.[15]

Steve Jobs' ability to give demos was magnificent and fun. In January 2007, Steve Jobs took out his iPhone and dialled Starbucks in San Francisco. He was concluding his iPhone demonstration about how to put Google Maps to work. He searched for a nearby Starbucks store and from the dais of the conference, called them. 'Good morning', answered the polite voice of employee, 'How may I help you?' 'Yes, I'd like to order 4,000 lattes to go, please', Jobs then said, 'No, just kidding. Wrong number. Goodbye!' As Jobs hung up, the audience burst out laughing. His call became the first public phone call made from an iPhone.[16]

The last, of course, in any presentation is the 'wow' factor. What would the audience leave with or a single thing that they would always want to remember? Keld Jensen suggests four ways to deliver the 'wow'. First by being the smartest speaker, second by aiming at winning the hearts of the audience, third by shocking the audience and last by generating positive energy.[17] Brian Tracy, for example,

---

[15] SendGrid Team, 'The 4 S's of a Good API Demo,' *SendGrid*, 17 October 2014, https://sendgrid.com/blog/4-ss-good-api-demo/ (accessed on 28 May 2019).

[16] Austin Carr, 'Because of Steve Jobs's First Public iPhone Call, Starbucks Still Gets Orders for 4,000 Lattes,' 3 April 2013, https://www.fastcompany.com/3006147/because-steve-jobss-first-public-iphone-call-starbucks-still- (accessed on 28 May 2019).

[17] Keld Jensen, 'WOW Your Audience! Four Ways To Deliver Masterful Presentations,' *Forbes*, 30 May 2012, https://www.forbes.com/sites/keldjensen/2012/05/30/wow-your-audience-four-ways-to-deliver-masterful-presentations/#1131b19e585e (accessed on 28 May 2019).

suggests connecting with the audience, linking to the opening of the talk and relating to the interest of the audience.[18]

The wow factor has been used by Apple's co-founder Steve Jobs innumerable times. Jobs in one of his presentations at during Apple's annual shareholders meeting took the stage, reached into a bag and pulled out the Macintosh. He turned it on and inserted a floppy disk.

The Mac introduced itself by saying the following:

'Hello, I'm Macintosh. It sure is great to get out of that bag. Unaccustomed as I am to public speaking, I'd like to share with you a maxim I thought of the first time I met an IBM mainframe: NEVER TRUST A COMPUTER YOU CAN'T LIFT! Obviously, I can talk, but right now I'd like to sit back and listen. So, it is with considerable pride that I introduce a man who's been like a father to me... STEVE JOBS.'[19]

This demonstration became one of the most popular and a brilliant technique to create a wow factor, viewed on YouTube by millions of people ever since then.

ANSWERING QUESTIONS

No one ever complains about a speech being too short!

—Ira Hayes

The question and answer session holds a vital key in clarifying points, reinforcing some of the main ideas, substantiating with further examples, clearing any misconceptions or misunderstandings or simply repeating. It is also important because first the speaker gets into a difficult zone and second the audience participates.

---

[18] Brian Tracy International, '8 Public Speaking Techniques To Wow Your Audience,' Brian Tracy International, https://www.briantracy.com/blog/public-speaking/tips-to-wow-a-crowd/ (accessed on 28 May 2019).

[19] Chris Hauk, 'Happy 35th Birthday to Apple's Original Macintosh,' Mactrast, 24 January 2019, https://www.mactrast.com/2019/01/happy-35th-birthday-to-apples-original-macintosh/ (accessed on 28 May 2019).

Many speakers, for example, allow questions at any point of time during the speech. While this is okay, this may break the flow of your presentation. However, this invites a lot of participation from the audience and there is a healthy discussion. If you are inviting questions at the end, you may be asking the organizers to collect the questions before you start your talk. You may choose to answer a few. You can also set it open for the participants to ask questions. In some cases when you cannot take up all the questions, ask the participants to connect with you over email or telephone. Tell this to the audience beforehand, 'I would be taking questions at the end of the presentation.' Some ground rules to answer these questions: First do not answer if you do not know. If you do not know the answer, just say, 'Sorry, I do not know' or 'I will need to check before I answer this.' Second avoid answering questions that divert the audience from the topic or which are too sensitive to be handled, such as personal information or an issue or something unrelated to the topic. You can say, 'We will take this offline' or 'Sorry this question is not pertinent to the discussion we just had.' Third listen before you answer. As a speaker, especially when we have presented the topic multiple times, we can gauge the question. This might be a fallacy of judgement. Listen to what is being asked; if you do not understand, ask them to repeat. Fourth you can encourage more questions by saying, 'I look forward to any more questions that you may have.' You can also thank by saying, 'Thank you for asking this question.' Fifth if there are a large number of people in the audience, you can repeat the question for the benefit of all. For example, 'What this gentleman has asked was ....' Last accept questions from different parts of the audience.

When you answer the questions, be precise and confident. A positive body language and an eye contact will match your confidence. Respond them as crisply as possible. You can choose to limit the questions that are asked. Handle disruptions well. People often start talking while someone is asking question or in between two questions. The best way to handle this is a small 'pause'. However, you can also ask the audience to remain quiet. For example, 'You will not be able to hear if there is noise in this room.' If you get a recording of your speeches, check on how you have fared and things that you need to improve upon.

CONCLUSION

Be still when you have nothing to say; when genuine passion moves you, say what you've got to say, and say it hot.

—D. H. Lawrence

Presenting is an art, and the greatest challenge that you face is capturing the minds and the heart of the audience. This does not come easy and what is required is great planning, execution and practice. The more you do, the more self-aware you become, thereby improving how you do the next time. Do not forget to analyse where you went wrong and what could have been improved after every presentation.

9 Be HOT: Honest, Open and Trustworthy

Alone we can do so little; together we can do so much.

—Helen Keller

GREAT COMMUNICATION, GREAT TEAMS

Chitra was a bright student during her MBA days. Her success came from her ability to work hard. Her motto in life was to be the best in whatever she did. The rigour in MBA to work as a team never hit her. She was busy showcasing her talent throughout, unwilling to leave an inch of space for her colleagues. She felt that the only way to succeed was through differentiating and marketing yourself. Things changed when she joined an information technology MNC as a management trainee. She was trained and deployed in projects. A new project came up for the organization and she was chosen to be a part of this work. The team had about 15 people, working both onsite and offshore. Her manager, a seasoned practitioner, did not want any trouble during the deployment of the project. However, during this time, Chitra was busy showcasing her work to the client and the manager. There were many instances when she surpassed her manager and interacted with the clients on issues that mattered. While the protocol suggested internal discussions, she avoided discussing with her manager. Many a times, her manager came to know about certain aspects from the client, which ideally should have been shared by Chitra. Emails and communications shared by the client/her manager were not passed to the team members and neither were important communications about the tasks at hand. While Chitra was given a feedback to mend her ways, she did not take it very seriously. At the final deployment of the project, when things started getting critical, Chitra sought help from her colleagues. This was the stage when all need to sit together to make things move, and get things up and running. By now things had started getting very bitter with her other team members. People refused help as they were well aware of her earlier motives. They shunned Chitra and refused to consider her as a part of their team. Although earlier Chitra had received a feedback from her colleagues to be more participative, she turned a deaf ear to all of these. In the last phase, after the project got launched, the team organized a success party with their managers. Although Chitra was called for the party, everyone prayed for her exit from the team.

What is easier than three people sitting together, meeting up and solving a problem? Probably, nothing. While this may seem to be easy, working in groups is really difficult. With cultural diversity, virtual work environment, 24×7 working environment, different time zones and different languages, the challenges have become bigger. The need to perform fast is the norm for most of the organizations and teams are becoming the model of working in organizations both in the public and private sector. Performance demands have risen sharply in both public and private sectors. 'Silos' are working no more and people in organizations work in more than two teams. However, at the same time, they need to act quickly. The path to success lies in the art of communicating in teams. Unless teams discuss with the key stakeholders and within themselves, there is no chance of survival.

The world is moving real fast today, and with plenty of technology, messages and communication channels, it is really hard to communicate clearly. Messages that are intended for people often do not reach them in time, resulting in unprecedented delays for teams and individuals.

One of the learning and development heads of an organization sent a mail to his next line of reportees about a global recognition that the department had received, asking them to send the message across to all the employees. When this gentleman came to talk to his employees in New Delhi, he casually mentioned about this award. To his surprise none of the people in the audience knew about this award. His email had not reached them.

Another bigger challenge is handling virtual teams. Today, you work in environments where the diversity of employees and the physical distance is tremendous. For example, in global deployment of information technology/consulting projects, you could be working with people in more than three to four time zones, and a majority of them are those whom you have neither seen nor met. You will be coming from a cultural background significantly different than the rest of your team members. This makes misinterpretation easy, only to be recognized later (sometimes days later), which causes tremendous frustration and rework. Misinterpretations are a popular breeding ground for chaos and conflict. Coupled with cultural and language challenges, this becomes even more difficult. Whether you like it or not, they are a reality today.

In one of the projects with a Chinese client, one of the team members said, 'It is very difficult to understand what he means on the phone. We do some work and it comes back with a request for change, inviting more rework. At the end of the day, both are terribly frustrated.'

Working with teams, sitting in close proximity or in far-off lands, organizations globally face this challenge and it is important to recognize the need to communicate effectively. Abundant or scarce information, unclear and ambiguous information are all the right reasons for a failure in communication in teams.

Communication in teams is further challenged because of the following. First is the interpretation of the meaning. Since we cannot understand what a person said really means (by going down his brains), we interpret it conveniently according to our understandings. If your team member says, 'It is done', you interpret it that the task has been completed. However, for slightly longer communications, the chances of misinterpretation remain. Second is that communication remains contextual. What it means in one circumstance, may not be in another.

Amit was given a feedback to follow the instructions carefully after an appraisal discussion. From the next cycle onwards, he started making notes of everything that his manager said. After a conversation got over, he used to clarify his doubts. While this was a good practice, no one really bothered till he started doing this for his customers. He started making notes (literally by the second on what had been said) and in case the clients raised issues with the work that was delivered to them, he used to send scanned copies of his notes to the client, trying to prove them wrong.

Third is that we send and receive messages at the same time. While we are talking to multiple people, we are also receiving multiple messages. For groups it becomes a challenge as all the members tend to interpret it the way they want to. Fourth group dynamics also play a role in how communication is done in teams. For example, when the sales manager is communicating with the team for higher targets, the group dynamics play a role. The sales team can already surrender to the idea that it is unachievable. Fifth unclear definition of roles could become a challenge to communication. If a project manager is unclear on what he wants from each of his team members, the quality of work would suffer. Sixth when team members represent different cultures, they are bound to clash to achieve their objectives. Coming from high- and low-context cultural backgrounds, communication could be really difficult.

Venky, a project manager, was a sceptical person. When he wanted something to be done, he would want an email to be written as a proof of it. However, when he wanted to communicate, he would prefer to talk as it did not have any legal implication or could not be raised in case there were issues later. Latin American countries, for example, are slow to go ahead with their deals. They take time to build relationships. Japanese believe in closed discussion. An Arab would always prefer to deal with a local partner and an American would be upfront about what they want from you.

The last challenge is the problem of bringing the 'elephant' into the room. Teams avoid discussing things that are uncomfortable or topics that are 'uneasy' for all or some because of certain personal or professional reasons. They find it uncomfortable to deal with things that matter to them and often remain 'silent' or just allow things to pass away, for example, a project going into red or a manager favouring a particular team member, giving and doing favours, and being honest, open and transparent to some of them.

What makes teams very unique is the collaborative spirit of a team versus individual performance. An important aspect of teams is the 'political correctness' with which we communicate. Although our minds are full of things that we want to speak up, we talk only what sounds pretty and music to the listener's ears. We play to the tunes of people often out of a need to do so or out of fear of being rebuked or deprived of an opportunity for growth.

You therefore play a critical role in the success of the team. The role could be of either a team player or a leader. You also need to switch over from one role to another depending on the situation. For example, you are a manager. You are a leader. However, when you are discussing strategy of your company with your superiors, you become a team player. So for most this is an interchangeable role.

COMMUNICATING TO BECOME SUCCESSFUL

If a team has to succeed, the team members' role cannot be undermined. Teams become our second family, sometimes for shorter durations or very long ones. They become a source of our learning, strength and support. Being part of great teams is sometimes what people aspire, however we behave contrary in failing teams. Whatever may be the reason for failure, we tend to keep away from such teams.

Let us start from the beginning, that is, when you join a new team. The first few days are the days of observation. You observe and make mental notes of things happening around you. You observe how people dress, the degree of formality, hierarchies, culture, talking, behaving, writing etiquettes and so on. The best way therefore is spending most of the time in listening to your colleagues and managers. In the initial days, talking should be minimal.

Rohith used to work in a family-owned business. While writing emails, he used to address everyone with 'Dear Sir'. After a couple of years, he joined an MNC and the first email he wrote, addressed the person as 'Dear Sir'. Nothing wrong though, the recipient responded back asking Rohith to address him by his first name, mentioning, 'Rohith, you are making me sound too old. We do not conform to this culture in our organization.'

Being a part of a new team is not easy. It is often objected by many for several reasons.

One of the managers in an organization was trying to expand his team. But his next line of managers felt that there was insufficient work for a new person. Although objected by others, a new person was hired. The new person had to face a lot of initial trouble to get recognition. Finally, after a year he was accepted by his colleagues.

While many teams introduce new team members or ask them to send out emails, many teams do not. You need to walk around or drop an email introducing yourself. In all cases, ensure that you do not over-communicate. Be very precise while you are introducing yourself to others. Spend time exploring one another. While talking to your peers, choose topics which are safe and help you learn. If you do not understand anything, clarify, like, 'Can you please repeat what you just said?' or summarize by saying, 'Let me cross check with you if my understanding is correct.' The first few days are the days of hand-holding. People around you will be supportive in most cases. However, there are the rude ones as well. Be aware of them. Ensure that you use your sense of humour or diplomacy to stride past them. For example, one of my colleagues was asked to photocopy papers. In such cases be assertive and refuse unless absolutely required.

Three things you must do at this stage. First listen to people, second summarize what has been said for a better understanding and the third is to ask questions to clarify—not too many of them but as many that help you get clarifications about your work. Keep talking to people, but do not get close to sub-groups or start politicizing or discussing anything about the organization.

I have had chances of encountering many people who from the first day took opportunities to bend the rules. They found out what works for them and what does not. You will find that these team members will land you in bitter zones and ensure that you either use your humour or diplomacy to tackle such issues.

A new joinee had started showing some personal interest in another colleague of hers. While she approached this guy, he realized something was wrong. He came to office the next day with some chocolates and gave it to everyone in the office as well as her. He mentioned the reason as his marriage anniversary.

Communicate assertively with people who take undue advantage of you. You can say, 'I am sorry, but I will not be able to do this now.' Some other assertive lines would be, 'Thank you for presenting this, but I would disagree with you on some of these areas' or 'Thank you for your suggestions. I will be considering them for my next presentation.'

Saying a no does not harm. It gives an indication that you will not be able to cater to the whims and fancies of people who try to dominate or over-influence you.

Rajat had just joined when his colleague came to him and said, 'Boss has asked you to do the presentation and get it checked by me.' Rajat understood that his boss had not asked him to. He said, 'Okay, can you please ask him to drop me a mail. I did not hear anything from him about this.'

Saying a 'no' always has its own challenges. You would virtually never want to say a no to your manager and saying a no to your team members go against you. Say a 'no' but in a way that does not hurt the other person. For example, 'Can I do that tomorrow?' (when you know his deadline is for today) or 'I am busy with some task at hand. Can this be postponed for later?' Or push it on to your boss if you share a good rapport with him. 'Can you please inform my manager that I will be working on this, marking me a copy in the email?' Some cases, however, need a direct no. In case you can direct the person to someone else who can help out, please do so.

When you ask people for a help, adopt a direct approach. A direct approach starts with a 'buffer statement', like, 'Hi Arun, my manager has told me to get the reports till date in a particular format.' Followed by your question, 'Arun can you please guide me to the person who can help me with the reports?' You can close this with a neutral statement like, 'Since you have done this before, do you have some suggestions or templates for me which will guide me through this?' Similarly, when you have been asked to help others or you do it voluntarily, use your listening skills effectively.

Before your feet are firmed on the ground within a new team, making unreasonable requests are a no-no. Your communication with your colleagues should be pleasant, open and honest. Do not discuss things that do not matter, like, 'I heard that Arun has been divorced. What is he doing now?' or organizational policies, 'This company is not going to give us anything more than this.' If you do not know anything, ask for help.

If people seem to be busy, reach out to your manager for help, for example, 'Can you please direct me to someone who could guide me with this?' Do not blow yourself up or rebuke people. Avoid bullying people or getting bullied by others. If you need to report, please do.

You should not be perceived as a person who is becoming a baggage for the team. Communicate on what you have done. Lay down the tasks that have been given, things that you have done or could not do and the help that is needed to do those tasks.

Another aspect is to take initiative to do a work. If something is not getting done, it is for you to figure out. If still it is not happening, reach out to your manager and all the people concerned. Set a meeting to discuss. Ask you manager for suggestions and be direct with your request. For example, you can say, 'I got in touch with the vendor, but he is not able to provide me with the data I am looking for. Do you have some alternatives for this? Or can you suggest something?' Be confident and assertive while you talk to people. For example, 'Hi Arun, I wanted to check if you are ready with the report? I will need a draft copy by today evening.'

SKILLS GOOD LEADERS NEED

Talent wins' games, but teamwork and intelligence win championships.

—Michael Jordan

'With great powers come great responsibility' (movie *Spiderman*; 2002). Our role as a team leader or a manager comes with certain degree of responsibility and power. Doing what you could possibly do as a team player is now difficult as a leader. There are people who are looking up to you. You will have to overcome challenges for your team members, help them understand the purpose, goals and their roles, build capability, look at their personal and career growth and support learning for individuals. You also need to help them adapt to organizational change. These are some of the tasks cut out for you apart from your deliverables. You will have to therefore mentor or coach them, facilitate discussions, resolve conflicts and ensure synergy amongst the team members. Doing this requires a lot of personal capabilities and skills. However, some skills pertaining to communication are your ability to be honest, transparent and open to your team members. You need to be direct, diplomatic at times and also maintain a high degree of personal integrity and a very good sense of humour.

The first biggest task cut out for you is to build a *synergy* amongst the team members and a great working relationship. It is an absolute must for every team member and to do this you will need to effectively communicate.

The first step is to be honest, open and trustworthy. Honesty is being open to your team members, making them realize what is possible or not possible from your end.

Kailash, a manager, knew his constraints. After a performance appraisal discussion, he had limited amount of bandwidth on what he could do. He did his best. It was impossible to keep everyone in his team happy. Kailash was honest about it. He used to be upfront and mention what could/could not be done. If he could not hike the salaries beyond a certain percentage, he used to say it upfront. If he could not give someone a promotion, he was clear about why he could not give. Although it did hit the team members initially, they used to recognize his challenges later.

To communicate *honestly* as a leader, it is best to be direct. For example, 'This is the best I could do.' Or say things like, 'I hope you are aware of the organizational mandates. I will not be able to promote more than two people. I have chosen them and not you, because...' (give them the reasons). While honesty is rated as the number one quality that leaders should possess, research done by PR firm Edelman finds that leaders fail miserably in this.[1]

You must be able to talk and mean the same.

A senior leader was addressing some new group trainees who had just joined the company. He was talking about all great things happening in the company and to him. He was painting a rosy picture of things and careers around them. A lot of other people senior employees were also sitting with them. A conversation was overheard after the meeting got over, '70 per cent of what he said are pure lies. I do not understand what is the reason to lie when these people will figure out the truth themselves within some time.'

The second biggest quality is to be *open*. Being open minded with people, ideas, suggestions, cultural values and eco-systems is needed.

---

[1] Michael Bunting, 'Honesty: The Single Most Important Leadership Value,' *CEO Magazine*, 4 March 2016, https://www.theceomagazine.com/business/management-leadership/honesty-the-single-most-important-leadership-value/ (accessed on 19 May 2019).

If you are unable to 'hear the truth', you should not be a team leader. If you are not able to withstand something which you do not value or do not confirm to, and you are not being open about it, you do not qualify to become a leader. One of the easiest way to say this, 'I do not know. Can I check and get back to you about this?' Other ways to communicate openness are to share all the information needed at work. Rather than saying, 'How stupid can you be?' Ask the question, 'So what do you think went wrong?' or 'How could have done this better?' or you could say, 'Thank you for suggesting. Let me seriously look into this.'

The third trait needed is the need to be *trustworthy*. In the book, *The Four Agreements*, authored by Don Miguel Ruiz, the first important touchpoint to lead a fulfilling life is to 'be impeccable with your word.' Imagine your people not trusting you with what you say. Teams do not work under pressure. Each of your team member has their individual thought process. To create a synergy, therefore, you must first be trustworthy. Speak with integrity. There should be no reason for your team members to doubt you. Even if you are talking tough with your team, but the team listening to you trusts in what you say and do, things will become easier. When you are talking to your people inspire them. Use sentences like, 'Yes, we can do this together.' or 'The word "impossible" does not exist in my dictionary.' or 'I know all the challenges, but can we collectively think about the solution.' Speak with excitement and your heart.

Be passionate about how you communicate. To create a significant impact, convey your messages clearly and concisely. If you are not speaking in a way that your audience will understand, you'll never get through to them. Narrate your stories. If people reverberate with them, you will be successful in getting through.

Nitin led a fairly large team. One day, he called his team and said, 'Look...I know this is odd to ask. But I am in an awkward position. The senior management wants this data immediately by the end of the day. I tried to negotiate the timelines but they are not in agreement with me. Please do not ask me the logic or why should we be doing this leaving all our work, but I am requesting all of you to leave aside all you work and do this for me.' The work got done. We stopped all our work. Divided ourselves into groups and finished it off way before the end of day.

Empathize with your people. Tell them, 'I know how difficult it is for you. Let me know how I can help you with this. Just as you expect them to trust you, you should reciprocate in a similar way. Listen to your people. It is also a great way to build trust. Do not interrupt them.

Another aspect of becoming a successful team leader is to ask 'powerful and relevant questions'. 'How do you think this is going to work?' rather than, 'Why is it not working?' or 'What are the things that you tried to do to complete the task?' rather than, 'Why was this not done?' If you feel that discussions in a team are going haywire, bring them back by saying, 'Can we get back to this topic later?'

VERBAL AND NON-VERBAL COMMUNICATION IN TEAMS

Teamwork is the ability to work together toward a common vision. The ability to direct individual accomplishments toward organizational objectives. It is the fuel that allows common people to attain uncommon results.

—Andrew Carnegie

Refer to the chapters on writing skills, conversations and non-verbal communication in this book. Apart from them, I am proposing some other points that you must consider while communicating in groups.

First have a purpose for every communication that you do. Write or talk to your team with an objective. Establish what you want your team to know or start discussing where you had left off in earlier meetings.

Second words have different meanings and how we use them matters a lot. So does the tone of writing. For example, writing, 'Do you know that new tall guy who has joined from Bangalore last week?' or the 'Fat lady at the reception' or 'The handicapped guy'. TED speaker and language historian, Anne Curzan, has some examples. 'Nice', for example, used to mean 'silly, foolish and simple' earlier, but today it is a compliment.[2] Therefore, choose words with care.

Third make it easier for people to understand. 'The client satisfaction survey tells us that we have got 4.5 on a scale of 5 and the client rated us as follows....' This means nothing. It does not tell you neither what you did great nor does it tell you the areas of improvement. So everything that you write or say should not be symbolic. Explain to your audience why it matters to them or what it means.

Fourth facts, inferences and opinions are different. When you talk or write your audience, specify what you mean. Are you stating a fact backed by data or an inference that you interpret of the data or an opinion what you believe in?

Last use humour cautiously. Neither avoid it nor over-use it.

I was talking for a 300+ gathering. In that I made a statement to lighten the environment. I said, 'One Bengali is lonely, two Bengalis are best friends and three Bengalis mean politics.' After my talk got over, two girls approached me telling they were thoroughly offended by my statement and being a Bengali myself, how dare I say that and demean the community. I realized it was a bad day for me. I was talking to another group later and used this example to tell them, 'How humour could backfire'. To this one of the professors said, 'You should have changed it to mean better. You could have said, "One Bengali, orator, two Bengalis, best of friends and three Bengalis, revolutionaries."'

Non-verbal communication supplements your verbal communication. A cheer on the face or a big smile means a lot. People would love to work with you. They would be happy to interact. If our face does not show willingness, then your colleagues or team members may

[2] TED Guest Author, '20 Words That Once Meant Something Very Different,' Ideas.TED. Com, 18 June 2014, https://ideas.ted.com/20-words-that-once-meant-something-very-different/ (accessed on 19 May 2019).

back out. Eye contact is essential. We reduce eye contact when we convey bad news. People with whom you maintain eye contact frequently feel more empowered than others. It is not only about the message, but how it is being said. For example, take a simple sentence like, 'I spoke to my manager today and the outcome was not pleasant.' Read this sentence by stressing on different words. You will find that it means differently every time. Our body language, gestures, what we hear, and use of our hands, fingers, palms and head all mean a lot while you are talking with your team. Your voice, for example, over the phone speaks a lot about you. You may appear cheerful or sound boring, disinterested or happy. For example, sitting open armed versus closed could have positive as well as negative connotations. Keeping people waiting or showing your importance by walking in late are part of chronemics. Not giving time to others or spending less time with people could be a sign of disinterest or busyness.

Use non-verbal communication effectively as a means to *emphasize* by stressing on a particular word or repeating a word; *reinforce* by patting on the back for a good job done; apart from what you have said, *supplement* by dressing appropriately for the occasion to appear confident and *substitute* by raising your hands up for supporting a statement or a comment.

FEEDBACK IN TEAMS

> Great teams do not hold back with one another. They are unafraid to air their dirty laundry. They admit their mistakes, their weaknesses, and their concerns without fear of reprisal.
>
> —Patrick Lencioni

Feedback is a critical process both for the team members as well as the leader. It does common good. While feedbacks tell a lot about things that need improvement, it helps provide corrective course of action. The first rule of feedback is to keep an open mind and environment. If a feedback is being given and you keep telling yourself that this is not right or you ignore it, you are not open to take a corrective action.

While this may be okay in certain circumstances, it is incorrect in most others. When a feedback is given, ensure that it is positive as well as negative. When I say, 'negative', I mean constructive criticism such as 'Tell us three things that were good and three that needed improvement.'

A senior manager of a company was given a feedback that he does not make an eye contact while he is talking to his subordinates. He looked at some of the recordings and realized that this needs to be corrected. Had he ignored, he would not have been able to take a corrective action.

First, the right way to give a feedback is to be constructive. Not giving a feedback or giving a feedback to please the ears of a person is never helpful. While you are being constructive, ensure that you do not judge the person, exaggerate or label them, for example, 'I did expect this as you have done this in the past as well. Nothing new about it.' Use facts to provide constructive feedbacks, for example, 'A corrective action in the mid-year would have helped when the figures were not reaching the targeted action.'

Second, use 'I' rather than 'you'. Rather than saying, 'You were late to the meeting', it is better to say, 'I feel that all the team members should be present when the meeting starts.'

Third, tell them how you felt and what you want them to do, for example, 'I did not expect this from my team members and would have at least expected a more proactive approach to solving this problem.'

Fourth, never argue. Look for a solution, for example, 'I have specifically told you not to take work from home without informing me.' The person on the other side starts the argument. You counter that by not arguing further, instead say, 'What do you think is the solution to this problem. The senior management is very clear on the guidelines to take work home.' Instead if you say, 'I will report this' will further the argument without any direction or purpose.

Fifth, feedback is not a monologue. Hear the other person out and counter his responses with what was possible, for example, the person responds, 'This was not possible', you should respond as, 'What were the challenges you saw in implementing this? Did this necessitate a discussion between us and some other team members'

Last never bring up topics which are irrelevant or which do not discuss the current issue at hand. Bringing past issues makes the situation tense and brings in resistance. Do not discuss things which are out of context, but state facts. Discussing things out of thin air rarely helps. Never give a person any feedback without data points.

ACTIONIZE THE FEEDBACK

What about teams and their members who receive feedback? It is time for them to actionize it. Note it down and take corrective action.

A senior manager had asked all the people, including his managers, to give feedback to anyone that he/she wanted to. This team had about 7 managers and about 23 junior team members. The feedback would remain anonymous and had to be dropped in a box with only the name of the person for who it was given. This was opened after a month and the feedbacks were given to the individuals. A particular member received the maximum feedback asking her to tone down her voice and attitude, show empathy and be humane towards every-one in the department. After reading this, she could not believe that is how people perceive her. She started working on it and after a year there was a dramatic transformation in her.

Thank people for their feedback. It becomes difficult for many people to listen to feedbacks that are being given. So let it rest for a few days before you start working on them. Listen while a feedback is being given and clarify if you have any doubts about the feedback. Try to understand what the person giving you a feedback means. Acknowledge what is right and what is wrong. Avoid arguments at any cost. However, at the same time, remember that taking corrective action for the feedback given to you is on you. If you are ignoring some of the feedback points given to you, be sure that you are not doing it as the cost of your personal and professional development.

MEETINGS ARE NECESSARY EVIL

Coming together is a beginning, staying together is progress, and working together is success.

—Henry Ford

We do not like meetings. But still team members are so engrossed in day-long meeting that sometimes it becomes impossible to talk to and meet people. Meetings are the biggest 'time wasters'. However, if done properly, they can be productive. Many times you will find people coming out of a meeting wondering about the purpose of the meeting. The better we understand meetings, the better it is for them to be productive and in proper light. Sometimes meetings get misdirected by few people, participants start getting bored and non-participative. Ultimately some use meetings to settle down scores with others, some use it to rebuke others, while very few use them productively to achieve a goal or a purpose. The most important thing to remember is to look at meetings from a professional standpoint. While some of the important aspects of a meeting need to be kept in mind, such as arranging for a venue, inviting the right people, having a purpose, having an agenda, following up and channelizing the meetings in the right direction, how we communicate in meetings is also an area that needs deliberation.

If you want to understand how difficult meetings are, have a casual discussion over coffee and see how difficult it becomes to keep people on track. In a meeting, all have their own agenda. Some come to kill their time, some hide behind a pillar in the hall, some keep checking their mobile phones, messaging one another or giving missed calls to others sitting in the same meeting and playing other pranks. Some talk a lot, some do not, some need to be coerced, some take up the entire show and many more. Some people have the tendency to hijack every meeting, taking the meeting to a different direction. You will therefore need to communicate in a manner that keeps the discussion focused, productive and participative. At the end of it, the meeting should have met its objectives.

Albert Einstein's said:

If I had an hour to solve a problem and my life depended on the solution, I would spend the first 55 minutes determining the proper question to ask…for once I know the proper question, I could solve the problem in less than five minutes.

Therefore, start with a right and clear agenda. Let the participants know what is expected from them. This can be sent out before a meeting or at the start of it. Invite the right people and ask them to do their homework. During the meeting, follow the general guidelines of communicating. Listen to people, maintain eye contact, ask the right questions, respect the opinion of others, be clear with your thoughts and ideas, do not be a show off or a hijacker of the meetings. Present your points with precision.

You could be requesting for information from the other members like, 'Can you please tell us what happened on the particular day' or 'Do you suggest any evidence of the same?' Similarly, you could be providing information like, 'I have read…' or 'During the course of my field work….' If you are summarizing, you can ask, 'Let me reiterate, if my understanding is correct…' or 'Now that we have understood the challenge at hand….' If you feel that your understanding is incorrect, you can ask, 'Did you mean….'

Negotiating, for example, would be another aspect of team meetings. For example, 'Can we all agree to these points?' or 'How many of us in the room agree to what has been said?' or 'I would like to hear about what others have to say about this.'

While you are participating in discussion, encourage people by saying, 'It was wonderful hearing all of you.' You may want to cheer the participants, like, 'It was a wonderful job done till here.'

As an individual team member participating, avoid sabotaging meetings, putting your ideas and thoughts ahead of others, not listening to people and disagreeing with everything. Do not show off what you have done, but be focused on the agenda of the meeting. Smile through the meeting and ensure you complete the task assigned to you at the end of the meeting. Provide an update to all.

CONCLUSION

In today's complex business environment, teams are necessary. Silos are now gone, and it is for everyone to prove themselves and work together as team members and leaders. Communication becomes an essential aspect of becoming an ideal team member. Similarly, your role as a team leader also focuses on the role of communication. Failures in teams are attributed to poor communication. Therefore, focus on communicating right and your team will become a high-performing team. As Mark Sanborn puts it 'In teamwork, silence isn't golden, it's deadly.'

10 Turning the Tables: Writing Effectively

*Read, read, read. Read everything—trash, classics, good
and bad, and see how they do it. Just like a carpenter who
works as an apprentice and studies the master. Read! You'll
absorb it. Then write. If it's good, you'll find out. If it's not,
throw it out of the window.*

—William Faulkner

UNDERSTANDING BUSINESS WRITING

Writing is and was never easy, and business writing is not about writing emails. These are the first two cardinal principles that you must remember, however with a disclaimer. Although writing is difficult, it can be mastered with some brain and heart, and writing is done for everything including correcting others, advertising copies, brochures, welcome notes, memos thank you notes, regret letters, funding letters, proposals, reports and finally our favourite emails.

Writing has two sides. The first is the science. There are some dos and don'ts which when followed give you some structure to the writing that you do. It lends the writing a basic shape which can be modified later. The art, however, is getting the writing right. It is about making the writing 'heart appealing' or something that touches the audience. Business writing is always for an audience. An audience which does not have time, is over exposed to different kind of readings and someone whose profile could be really diverse right from the executive to the CEO. We will therefore in this chapter first look at the science of writing and then the art of it.

The recent dependency of people on the use of various kinds of tools and technologies to make writing crisp and correct is a misnomer and highly overrated. No technology can ever make a piece of badly written junk into something adorable. It is the creativity of the writer that plays the key role in it. Poor writers also have their own set of inhibitions, called as procrastination and writers block, which come in their way. But a genuinely great way to be a good leader also lies in what you write. Writing expresses an implicit confidence in your audience and gives it a brand to engage with.

WRITING: STARTING WITH THESE FOUR PRINCIPLES

Writing is not easy. It is time consuming and you will always be unsure whether your audience has read your message. You should consider yourself very lucky indeed if you get some responses on your messages. It could a simple activity as asking for volunteers on a weekend to do a social service program. Remember that your audience is busy, diverse and over exposed. Your audience will have to find some time for to read the first few lines, (probably read it all), be engaged, feel the difference and act on what you really want them to do. That is a lot to ask.

The first principle is the principle of not writing. If you can do things over a telephone call or you can meet a person to get the things done, writing should be secondary. You can always follow up with a correspondence but treat writing as a secondary way to reach out to people. While this may not work always, this works miraculously well in some situations. If you want to send an unsolicited proposal, check if you can talk to the person to make it a solicited proposal. If you want to send an email to a group of people, see if you can teleconference them. If you want to talk to your HR about some documents that you want them to send, an email is better. It is also better to write when you would want to have a documented proof of a conversation. Therefore, choose your way. However, avoid the itch to write on the first go. Writing takes a lot of your quality time. Therefore, think before you choose to respond. Just because an email was sent to you, it does not imply that you will have to react or respond to the message. Choose and reply only to the ones which you feel need your attention and delete the ones which do not. If you respond to every other mail, you are being unproductive and criminally wasting your productive time on things that are trivial and do not add value to you or the organization.

When I worked for a very large organization, my manager always insisted that I go and talk to the senior managers to get my work done. I asked him, 'Why is it so?' He said, 'First is because you need to develop a rapport. Second no one knows you. You need to build an identity. Then you can do the way you want to. Third they receive at least 300 emails in a day. Why on earth should they act on what you are writing? Fourth they have other important things to do. Why should they leave their work to do yours unless they have a strong reason?'

The second principle of writing is a habit of reading. If you read well, it is quite probable that you will write well. Reading gives you a depth and writing helps you express. These are two great combinations, quite like the Britons love for fish and chips with tartare sauce. It just goes well. If you read, you get a hang of the style and this helps you understand what you need to write and how you need to express your thoughts and ideas. What do you read? Everything that you can lay your hands on. If you are serious about business writing, read stuff that closely relates to business. Look at the style, especially how they convey without exaggerating. Understand the latest happening in business and this goes a long way to great writing.

Spend some time to understand your audience and how you want to reach out to them is the third principle. If you know who they are, where they are and what you want them to do, a lot of work is done. If your audience is diverse, tackling them is a different game than tackling a more homogenous audience. First look for standards. If there is a company standard of responding or if someone has done something before, you can always build on that. For example, a template or a guide. Responding to a proposal, for example, could be a standard format that you may follow. That is the easiest. It saves a lot of time and effort. Second look at other ways of reaching them. If you can do a video conference or a teleconferencing, do that. If you can bring them to a room and talk, still better. However, choose the richest medium to reach them. If the groups are large and diverse, reach out to them using multiple channels. Ensure that they do not miss your message. At least ensure that they know what you intend to say or the least ensure that they are aware that something is happening about it.

Empathize with your audience is the fourth principle. Most of the senior managers that I have met have two complaints: 'I do not know what they want me to do' and the second biggest complaint, 'It is so technical and information loaded that the document is not worth looking at it.' You would have spent your nights writing the best report, but they had no time. Look from their perspective. They get so many things to read about. Why should they read yours when your writing was unclear, technically overloaded and they did not know what you wanted them to do. Complex writing skills filled with jargons rarely comprise good business writing. They have so much to read, write and take action on.

Business Writing: The Science

> Say all you have to say in the fewest possible words, or your reader will be sure to skip them; and in the plainest possible words or he will certainly misunderstand them.
>
> —John Ruskin

No one really wants to read a document. They just want to know what it says. Let me present you with 12 nuggets of writing wisdom which will help you accomplish your business goals in an effective manner.

Nugget 1: Do not waste time to get to the point. This is fairly simple. Do not waste the readers' time. If you are writing a direct message, get straight to the point. Do not keep the reader hanging around with things that he may not be interested in reading. Many people often merge two ideas like how is the person doing and something related to work. One idea for every writing or paragraph is what should be followed. Use bullets if needed to put down your thoughts or what is expected from the reader. In cases of unsolicited written communications, introduce yourself and come straight to the point.

For example, 'I have been thinking for quite some time about this and finally I came to the conclusion that this is the best way of getting out of this mess' can be made into, 'The best way to get out of this mess is....'

Nugget 2: Be clear—present complete information. Information which does not help the person reading the communication or the person asking for it is not worth writing. If you are informing about an accident that has happened in the factory and you have forgotten to write about the number of workers injured, then it is an incomplete message. Always remember that when you write, ensure that the reader is able to base his decision on it. When you want some information from someone, ask things which will make the communication self-explanatory without the need for further communication.

For example, 'I will be travelling by Indian Airlines, flight number AI 6789 and reaching the airport by 10.30 AM IST. Please organize the pickup accordingly' is incomplete writing. Instead write, 'I will be travelling by Indian Airlines, flight number AI 6789 on 17 May 2018 and reaching the New Delhi airport by 10.30 AM IST. Please organize the pickup accordingly.'

Nugget 3: Be crisp with words, sentences, paragraphs and your thoughts. Minimize the usage of the words, and therefore the size of your sentences and paragraphs. While this does not mean making your sentences 'choppy', but reducing the amount of words to express the thoughts in a similar way. If you can limit your words and sentences, it becomes easier for the readers to understand.

For example, 'I am sure you can be of great help in this situation and I look forward to your support. I will be reaching out to you in case of any emergency' can be rephrased as, 'I am sure of your help. I will be in touch.'

Nugget 4: Be precise. When you are writing, be clear on what you want the reader to do. Avoid being too general so that the reader is not left to guess or make a telephone call to understand what is expected. Readers who do not have the necessary time will send these emails to the recycle bin. Some more compassionate people will ask for a clarification.

Writing something like, 'Can you please send me the study material of HAN 121, 122, 123 and 124?' You act compassionate as the person who has sent you the email is in a different time zone. You respond back, 'Can you please tell me exactly which materials you want and the names of the material as there is a limitation on the size of the attachments?' To this the person replies, 'Please send HAN 121 and 122.' He does not give you the names. You am extremely tied up to search for the names as you have a million courses starting with these names and it is time consuming. You respond back. He takes another 24 hours to send you the names before you can give him access to the material.

Nugget 5: Avoid jargons. Limit the usage of jargons, especially when there are people outside your organization reading it. Even the jargons you use in your department may sound Latin to others in the same organization. What is acceptable to you is not for others. If you at all you need to, explain it in a line or two. Give meanings of the words and the context of usage in the appendix.

I recently received an email from my department saying, 'Please create a contest for the pilot test.' I was absolutely unaware of what it meant because I had received no communication on the latest process changes that had happened in the piloting. I had to call up the person who had sent me the email to understand the context and the new process, and only then I could do it. While this was something internal, do you think the readers who are not a part of your organization will have the time to understand your lingo?

Nugget 6: Check the usage of a word. No one is going to grant you an award for writing long and complex words. You do not stand to benefit. Nor do your readers. Use words that are simple and easy to understand. Rather than writing 'expedite' use of 'moving fast' helps in understanding better. Readers may not be educated enough to appreciate the words you have written. For them to refer to the meaning of a word to comprehend is a waste of time. Keep it simple. Words such as 'bewildered', 'ambidextrous' and 'garrulous' look fancy, but mean nothing for your readers.

Nugget 7: Edit and have a second look. Do not be in a rush to send it across. Give it a chance to rest. Give a second or a third look to it. Get other people to vet the document or work before you hit on the button. Messages with wrong punctuations, spelling errors and typos can be of sufficient embarrassment. Punctuations could be critical.

For example, you write: 'Woman without her man has no reason for living.' After this you give it to a woman, she punctuates this as, 'Woman: Without her, man has no reason for living.'[1] Or 'A panda eats shoots and leaves.' Now put a comma and see the change in the meaning. 'A panda, eats, shoots, and leaves' or 'A panda, eats, shoots and leaves' or 'A panda eats, shoots and leaves.'[2]

If they are numbers, be extra cautious about them. Readers who are good at their spellings, spot errors in the spellings early and those are the ones catch their eyes easily. Avoid over-reliance on computer spell checkers. However, ask someone to check the spellings if you are not confident.

A lady named Kamini had written me a mail. I responded back to her, and after some time she called me and blasted me on the phone. I could not understand why she did that. I asked her what the issue was all about. She said, 'Look at your email and you will understand' and banged down the phone. I looked at it for some time. I could not find any. I called my colleague and asked him to take a look. After 15 minutes of severe introspection, I saw that the spelling of her name, 'Kamini', was written wrongly by me as 'Kaminee', which changed the meaning of her name to a 'two-faced b$#*#' from 'someone who is beautiful'. I could only be sorry for myself.

---

[1] http://theliterarylink.com/punc.html (accessed on 26 May 2019).

[2] Lynne Truss, *Eats Shoots & Leaves: The Zero Tolerance Approach to Punctuation* (USA: Profile Books, 2003).

Have a conversational approach to writing: Write as if the person is conversing with you. When we converse, we say, 'Let me know if you need any help preparing the documents. I will do that for you.' However, the moment we convert this into a written form, we make this as, 'If you need any support for the aforesaid documents, which we had discussed, do let me know. I will definitely spare some time to do that for you.' What we say does not match with what we write and invariably we use more words while we write. So the easiest way to achieve this is by re-thinking and using only those words in your writing that you would do if you are meeting the person face to face.

Business Writing: The Art

Nugget 1: Keep your readers in mind. Your writing has everything to do with the readers. It is ultimately for the readers that you are writing for. Therefore, give them their due importance. Ensure that their reading is smooth, non-time consuming and that they get the complete or the desired information by reading. Try to ensure that you have tailor-made your message as much as you can. One size fits all cannot be the mantra. If you are responding to more complex queries like responding to a proposal, ensure you have responded to everything that had been asked for. Always ask, 'What will they get by reading this piece of information.' As Warren Buffett rightly summarizes it,

> When writing Berkshire Hathaway's annual report, I pretend that I'm talking to my sisters. I have no trouble picturing them: though highly intelligent, they are not experts in accounting or finance. They will understand plain English, but jargon may puzzle them. My goal is simply to give them the information I would wish them to supply me if our positions were reversed. To succeed, I don't need to be Shakespeare; I must, though, have a sincere desire to inform.[3]

---

[3] James Hurford, 'Warren Buffett's Guide to Writing in Plain English,' *Bizcommunity*, 1 February 2013, https://www.bizcommunity.com/Article/196/98/88472.html (accessed on 26 May 2019).

Nugget 2: Make it personal. The usage of 'I' is most misused in business writing. It is important to connect with the audience, and the use of 'we', 'our' and 'you' helps. These words keep the interest of the reader going. Also ensure that you use an active voice than passive. Rather than writing, 'It is recommended that we replace our instrument' which sounds impersonal, using, 'We recommend the replacement of our instrument' makes it more personal. Active verbs add more zing to your writing. Make it appear as if there is an individual behind the conversation and not an organization.

Nugget 3: Organize yourself better. A lot of planning goes before you sit down to write. Complex writings, especially long reports and responses to proposals, for example, require writing as a team. Assign the responsibilities to people and ensure that they are done. Follow standards to write them down. Even if you are writing as an individual, make a summary of what you intend to write and what you want to cover. An outline helps in putting down those ideas on paper. While you may not have the time to do this for regular pieces of writing, you may want to do this for the more critical ones. Also before writing, you may need to get information from different stakeholders and departments. Plan them in advance so that you do not need to hunt for them when you sit down to write.

Nugget 4: Ensure the flow; connect the ideas together. The ultimate idea of great writing is that you are effectively able to pass on the message to your audience. To do that, ensure the flow is correct and seamless. When you write a sentence of a paragraph, focus on not more than one or two ideas. If you want to push in more ideas, move to the next. Ensure that you transition the reader smoothly from one paragraph to another and from one chapter to another. The sentences in the paragraph should also be very well organized ensuring completeness of the document.

TYPES OF BUSINESS WRITING

Platforms such as LinkedIn, WordPress and Twitter have placed billions of dollars in technology to give power into the hands of billions of writers entirely for free—something that once only belonged to major media and publishing firms. But technology cannot give the reader a sense of writing, which a book like this can. Let us empower ourselves with this knowledge and understanding the types of writing.

Business writing is primarily of three types. First are the routine messages, second are the persuasive ones and the third are the negative messages. Routine messages are those which the receiver would be receiving daily and are direct by nature. Our routine conversations are generally direct messages. The second type are the persuasive messages through which a person attempts to convince an individual or group to take certain specific actions. The person reading it may or may not be in agreement with what you are saying and he needs to be persuaded. For example, budgets for a foreign travel or additional budgets for sales promotion or a new project with requires more people. The third type is a negative message, also called as a bad-news message, conveys unpleasant information. It may disappoint, upset or even anger a reader. We need to say a 'no' but maintain the goodwill of the organization at the same time. For example, rejecting an idea, firing an employee, reporting the loss of a person or an employee, firing a vendor etc.

For *direct messages*, be clear about your objectives and state your request upfront, explain your requirement and close with the action that you want the reader to take. When you are writing *persuasive messages*, understand the objective of writing, know more about the audience. You then turn to writing: Gather attention, create interest and motivate your reader to act. For *negative messages*, you can either use a direct or an indirect approach. Direct approach is to present the bad news, provide an explanation and close on a positive note. The indirect approach is to provide a buffer statement to open, give reasons for the bad news, present the bad news or explain if needed and then close positively. In negative messages you can sandwich the bad news in between two buffer statements or neutral statements.

HOW TO START WRITING?

If you can't explain something simply, you do not understand it well enough.

— Albert Einstein

Writing has four distinct parts. The first is to gather information and divide the responsibilities. The second is to draw an outline which needs to be followed. The third step is to put down the thoughts to paper and the last step is to complete and close the process by checking for its quality and distributing the message. These steps are essential for a more complex writing process like responding to a proposal. However, in writing process which are simpler you will hover around the second, third and the fourth steps only. For routine messages, you will only be doing the third and fourth steps.

The first step is to gather information. While some of the information may be readily available, some may not. It sometimes become time consuming to hunt for the real information or data. Even within the same organization finding the necessary information may be of a big challenge. You may wish to divide your team into smaller units to collect the information. At this juncture assign the responsibilities to your team members from the start to the end of each of the activity that needs to be completed.

The second step is to draw an outline. Remember that clear writing is a result of a clear thinking process. The more clear you are with what you want to write, the better your final outcome is likely to become. You may choose to debate and draw an outline later or may have all the ideas put together first. It depends on the comfort level of the individual leading the process. For ideas, the best way is to brainstorm. You may also solicit for ideas outside your team or look at previous similar responses. You can also draw a 'mind-map' to tighten the brainstorming or put a flow to your thoughts and ideas, and design on what actually needs to be put in the writing and what need not be.

The third step is to put the thoughts down to paper. If you are doing this as a team, have a standardized guideline. However, if you are doing it individually, outline what you want to write or summarize it in the form of a couple of points. Write down the broader headings followed by the smaller ones and then logically re-organize the others. You may ask your manager to take a look or approve the format of writing. How do you start writing? The biggest challenge that every writer faces is 'procrastination'. The sheer idea of writing puts them off and they keep postponing this activity till the deadline is very near. Another challenge that comes is the writer's block which prevents the ideas flowing to the paper and the writer is unable to put down anything on paper. British writer Hilary Mantel has this piece of advice for such situations,

> If you get stuck, get away from your desk. Take a walk, take a bath, go to sleep, make a pie, draw, listen to music, meditate, exercise; whatever you do, don't just stick there scowling at the problem. But don't make telephone calls or go to a party; if you do, other people's words will pour in where your lost words should be. Open a gap for them, create a space. Be patient.[4]

There are different ways to get over this. One that I follow and strongly believe in is to keep writing bits and pieces every day. Write a page or two every day, allow it to rest and then revisit with a fresh perspective. You may choose to adopt any of the strategies which overcomes this block. Please do not keep editing in parallel to the writing process. The first few drafts may not be great and do not judge the final output. If you are getting stuck writing the difficult part, first handle the easier ones. This deviates the thoughts. Remember that it is your work and no one is more interested in it than you. No one is supposed to inspire you to write apart from you.

The last step is the most important step. You are now wrapping it up and you must ensure completeness of the writing and the purpose for which it was written. Edit it, put it for rest and then re-edit it.

---

[4] Hilary Mantel, 'Quotable Quote,' *The Guardian*, 25 February 2010, https://www.goodreads.com/quotes/444464-if-you-get-stuck-get-away-from-your-desk-take (accessed on 26 May 2019).

Multiple rounds of editing do not harm anyone. Give couple of the copies for others to read and suggest. Ensure that you are not making any major changes to your writing at this point. If there are some minor modifications or corrections suggested, please do them. Putting a document to rest and then revisiting it is a wonderful way to take a different look at the document. Avoid being in hurry to send across the document. If you are in a last minute rush, it means you have not planned yourself well. Check for the figures, tables, labels, references and the details that you have put in. Send the message to the right set of people or the audience it was intended for. Use the right ways and means to reach out to them or the ones prescribed like just 'sending out and email'.

EDITING AND IMPROVING READABILITY

Never ever send out any document without editing it. Good writers always focus on editing their documents as it is the most important activity and they follow a set of principles to give it a perfect finish. This is the step where you are garnishing your food or polishing your diamond before handing it over to your customer. Ensure every single way to make it look perfect and appealing. So how do you do it? First look at the science of writing. Ensure that you have made it crisp, precise and sharp. Trim down all the fat from the document. Check for all the possible mistakes especially with the numbers. Second check the order and see if the flow is established. The easiest way to do this is to find out if you are able to guide the reader from one thought to another. Third ensure completeness of the data and the information that you have provided. Revisit the facts and the opinions and check if you have presented them correctly. A half-baked document provides no outcome. It comes with further clarifications resulting in chaos at times. To do this look at the possible gaps or flaws that you're writing may have. Fourth proofread the document as many times as possible. Give it to a professional proofreader if required. Tighten up your language and make it active and personalized. Last ensure that you have read it or have asked others to read it from the perspective of the reader. You can try reading it backwards starting from the last paragraph or reading aloud each word. If you are sending it to others for taking a look, you may choose to accept them or reject their suggestions. In either cases thank them for taking the efforts. This should be your personal call. One of the other best practices I recommend is to read a document loud. This ensures correctness of the document.

The *three best practices* to be followed for editing are: first, hand over multiple copies to people for them to read and provide a feedback. Second, when you are doing it all alone, give some time for the document to rest after you have done the first round of editing. Third, hire a professional if the document is very critical.

How does the reader feel when he gets a first glance of your document? Is this going to be easy or difficult? If the case is former, a good amount of job is done. The reader is probably going to take a glance at your document. Your document therefore should have to be easy on your readers. Few things that can be done to improve the readability are: first, give margins and spaces around the document and use good quality paper if you are printing it. Second, keep your paragraphs short but ensure that you have provided lists, headings and sub-headings to make it look better and classified. Third, use underlining and italics only when required. Do NOT overdo it. Fourth, be careful with the usage of capital letters which denote shouting at your audience. Fifth, present your points as bulleted or numbered. Last, ensure consistency with your standard of writing—margins, size, typeface and space. Keep the design simple and allow 'whitespaces' in your document. It makes your document look great.

MANAGING EMAILS AND WRITING ETIQUETTES

All good writing begins with terrible first efforts. You need to start somewhere.

—Anne Lamott

Emails are a wonderful tool. Days when we were in school were about writing letters to people. It was time consuming, slow and costly.

The responses would take their own time and people had all the time to write letters. In fact, we focused on the writing than on the volumes of the letter we wrote. By the beginning of 2000 emails had hit. People starting hooking themselves at cyber cafes to get their email ids created and in the next decade to come emails replaced letters. They were fast, easy and cheap. There was no delay or need to deliver and the conversations could go on smoothly without any hitch. The receiver was at his own convenience and the sender too, and they could send or receive at any point of time. The email ids became our second address after our residential address. We had to quote it in everything that we did and it became a large part of our lives. However, along with this came a lot of challenge in our daily lives at the workplace.

On an average, I receive about 100 emails a day and on days I am unfortunate I receive about double of that. That takes me about four hours daily clearing them and responding to them as well as writing new ones. Once during screen sharing with my manager, I saw that his inbox had about a 1,000 odd unread emails. I was amazed. Though I had a hearty laugh then, later I realized it was not his fault. He just did not have enough time. And if you are coming back from a long vacation, only the almighty can save you. It goes on and on, and more the number of years you put into service, more would be volumes in your inbox, unread. While everyone is doing it and using it, the effectiveness is lost and no one takes it seriously or takes it for granted in many cases. We just do not read them. One of my colleague says, 'In any email where I am in cc and bcc, I delete them. That reduces my stress levels to an extent.'

However not all of these come without challenges. You may miss out on important messages and in many cases we overlook mails that have been sent. Sometimes even mails which are of use to us are ignored.

It was a bad time for a Mumbai-based MNC. One day the HR shot out a mail, with the subject: Changes to the calendar holidays from this financial year. Even before reading the mail, many employees started shouting, 'Here is another email to bother us.' In fact, quite the contrary. The company had increased the number of leaves for the employees.

A lot of short, long and collaborative writing is happening on emails. Although emails are not suited for larger writings or for a diverse audience, we seem to have significantly turned a blind eye to it. We want to make the email to be fit as a mode of communication for everything. I heard a senior manager saying, 'Emails are legally accepted by the law and our company. My job is to write and if they do not read and act, it is their headache.' Whether you like it or not,' he says, 'please read it. My job of communicating gets over after sending the email'.

Both the sender and the receiver have their own set of challenges. What do you do in such situations? The first that I suggest is to write less. When you come to the office in the morning, just do not start writing. Many people I see start writing as if they are into a life-saving drug of emails. If you can talk to sort out the issue, please do so. The second is do not wait for emails to hit your inbox. You are killing a lot of your productive time doing that. Many people keep staring at their inbox to check if they have received an email or not. Stop this and check emails only once or twice a day. The third is to make the subject line clear and crisp. You can set the tone of the email with the subject line. For example, 'Thank you guys'. Subject lines that are vague are unlikely to catch the attention of the reader. Emails cannot be differentiated. All look the same. You cannot differentiate unless the heading is catchy.

One of my colleagues had written an email with the subject line, 'Sex and the city: A new twist'. He had written this email to about 600 people. In the email he told about his journey with the organization and that it would be his last working day in the company. Like it or not, most of them had opened the email to read such a fantastic subject line in a conservative company. However, he was not reprimanded. His purpose was done.

I do not however suggest you to do that. Let me be honest. I delete half of the emails without even reading them. Some of them are auto directed to the junk folder. The fourth is to be crisp and to the point. I really mean crisp. The more words you spend, the readers become less interested. I expect to understand my emails after reading the first two sentences. Anything beyond that is not worthwhile. Anything that you have written should be cut down by about 60 per cent. The final draft should be less than a half of the original. The fifth is to follow the rules of good writing which we have explained earlier. I know it is a bad practice that I follow, but in many cases I write one-liners; I do not provide any salutations and do not put any signatures. I just can't afford to do that. It is a terrible practice. Please do not. Sixth never respond when you are angry or irritated or reply to something that has been bothering you. I have personally regretted writing 'nasty replies'. When I cool down, I feel different. Emails are not for fighting battles, winning them and loosing friends. You do not get anything by escalating issues. You create enemies and in organizations you come to achieve a common goal and not gather enemies around you. Seventh choose the right message that deserve your immediate attention. Avoid responding to all the messages. Give a thought to your responses. You can choose to leave them in a draft stage for some time before you hit the 'send' button. Eighth choose the right set of people who are supposed to receive the email. Do not keep adding people to the list. Avoid the usage of 'reply all' button. Ninth when you see an email chain going nowhere and all are adding to the ideas or repeating them in their own words or posing to be an intellectual, please put an end to it and call everyone for a meeting. Last remember that emails are not private, although we use official emails for personal purpose. They all can be made public and it may become the cause of an embarrassment.

GOLDEN RULES OF WRITING

1. Do not flag every message as urgent.
2. Do not change the subject line of a chain mail thread even if you are adding some new ideas.
3. Do not send mails with two different subjects using the same subject line.
4. Send separate emails for separate topics and ideas.

5. Close with a 'complete' signature.
6. If you are writing an unsolicited mail, try finding out who the right person is.
7. Avoid using smileys, exclamation marks, emoticons in emails or fancy backgrounds or weird colours or fonts.
8. Check if you have added the attachment if you have written PFA.
9. When you are not in office, set 'out of office' messages. This clears off the air on whom to get in touch in an emergency and when you could be responding back.
10. Never put people in 'bcc' without informing the recipients in 'cc' and 'to' know about it.
11. Use abbreviations in check. Usage of LOL, AFAIK, PFB, PFA, ROFL should be avoided.

Writing however has become a disappointment in today's business world. The new generation of people have started feeling that writing means technology. In the age of short communications, the very basics of writing have been forgotten and this has been the cause of major embarrassments at organizations. The basic science behind the writing of a communication is way behind any level of satisfaction. More and more of what is being written is being sent for rounds of editing before they are actually sent out to people. Managers are becoming highly 'insecure' of asking subordinates to draft messages as they are doing a lousy work.

Writing is an art and this comes only with good amount of practice. Reading will give you the necessary depth for being great, but it is ultimately the efforts that you put in to good quality writing. Remember that 'write less but (mean) more'.

BIBLIOGRAPHY

1. William Zinsser, *On Writing Well: The Classic Guide to Writing Nonfiction*, 7th ed. (New York, NY: Harper Collins, 2006).

2. Bryan A. Garner, *HBR Guide to Better Business Writing* (Boston, MA: HBR Press, 2012).

11 Call to Action

WHAT HOLDS US BACK?

P. C. Mustafa belonged to a small village in Kerala. His father was a coolie and mom was a homemaker. His village was deprived of almost everything; it had only one primary school which could be accessed only after walking for kilometres. Mustafa failed in class 6, however got a second chance to study. He never looked back again. He started off with his own venture, iD Fresh, selling idly and dosa batters, which now reaches more than eight Indian states and is also exported. Currently their revenue is over a billion.[1]

All of us face challenges in some form or the other and there are some factors that hold us back. Even in organizations, we face obstacles in various forms. While some surrender to the obstacles they face, some try to leave the struggle in between and others overcome the struggle after persistently trying to change.

As I had argued in the first chapter, there are tortoises and hares in the corporate world. Each has its own characteristics and they complement one another. The competition in the world around is cut-throat and you have minimal chances to escape. You cannot get away from the bell curve of performance; nor choose your manager or the work you do. Whatever the case, whosoever you are, we have to 'communicate' effectively and efficiently with everyone around us.

---

[1] Saraswati Singh, 'How This Coolie's Son Who Failed in Class 6 Built a 100 Crore Company?' The Hacker Street, 2019 https://in.thehackerstreet.com/p-c-mustafa-100-crore-company/ (accessed on 30 May 2019).

So what prevents us from improving on our communication skills? Primarily three factors: *lack of self-awareness, our fear/anxieties and habits.*

First is the lack of self-awareness. We feel that we do a wonderful job of communicating. But if we take a recording of how we speak and how we talk, we will be in for a surprise. One of my colleagues had commented,

Every time we receive an email from Mani, two people need to sit together to understand what she has tried to mean.' In another, John's reportee came to him and said, 'Look John…I am sorry but please remove me from reporting to Satya?' 'But why?' He said, 'John, he is so pathetic with his communication that he is neither able to understand what his customers are saying nor is he able to express what he has in his mind. We have landed up in serious trouble because of miscommunications between him and the client.

Most people feel that they are self-aware, (about 95%) but they actually are not (only 15% are) according to a research done by Professor Tasha Eurich. What this means is that we might 'feel' that we know ourselves, whereas in reality we don't.

In my experience, I have seen that people get jittery, irritated and sometimes upset about the opinions of others. They do not like others interrupting them, but are themselves okay when they do it with others. They pose their ideas, unwilling to listen to people or others in a team setting. This is an example of lack of self-awareness.

Self-awareness, however, helps in understanding ourselves better, thereby making us more confident and more likely to communicate effectively. In most cases of communication, we often do not realize that we interrupt while we speak, we message while someone is talking to us (we do not listen), we are not able to articulate our ideas, loose our temper while answering questions, force upon decisions on others in meetings or just write pathetically.[2] You are probably

---

[2] Tasha Eurich, 'Working with People Who Aren't Self-Aware,' *Harvard Business Review*, 19 October 2018, https://hbr.org/2018/10/working-with-people-who-arent-self-aware (accessed on 30 May 2019).

suffering from the 'CEO disease', identified by Professor Tasha Eurich. This disease is 'really' serious, which means that the higher you climb up on the corporate ladder, the lesser self-aware you become.[3] But why aren't we self-aware? First, we do not like to hear negative feedback about ourselves. Second the other person does not want to put us down by telling things that would not sound music. Professor Tasha Eurich sums up the behaviour of self-aware individuals as: poor listening, rebuttal of any feedbacks given, tailoring a message for the audience, high opinions about 'self', hurtful to others, love to credit themselves for success and blame others for failure.

Second, is the fear and anxiety that hold us back from communicating. 'Should I or should I not'? After sometime you say, 'Okay, let us leave this.'

A lady filed an anti-sexual harassment case to the internal committee of the company. She complained, 'I do not know this guy. This guy is stalking me, standing near my cubicle and disturbing me. I get calls from him….'There were many more allegations. The committee started its investigation. The boy was invited for a discussion and the committee came to know things that surprised them further. The boy said, 'We studied in the same university and were in a relationship. However, I had to break up due to some reasons, but she was unwilling. Although I tried to reason this out with her, she did not accept. I left it at that, taking this no further.' The investigation found evidences against the lady and she was fired from the organization. She said in her exit interview, 'I wanted to teach this guy a lesson.' While breaking up, had the guy informed his manager/ HR about this, he would have probably been spared from this harassment.

Tough conversations are our biggest fear. For some it is business writing, for others it is presenting or meeting new people and saying a 'hello'. We do not like offending or interfering. We therefore

---

[3] Joe Avella and Shana Lebowitz, 'You or Someone You Work for May Suffer from "CEO Disease"—And There's Only One Cure,' *Business Insider*, 16 May 2017, https://www.businessinsider.com/tasha-eurich-insight-ceo-disease-self-aware-2017-5?IR=T (accessed on 30 May 2019).

withdraw. So is the case when we write or talk or ask questions. Although there is an elephant in the room, we do not ask the questions that would bother all. We do not convey the right things, we do not tell our customers that a project is going to get delayed and so on. Fear and anxiety hold us back and we do not press ourselves into communicating with people. Fear, for example, 'I might be terminated from work,' or anxiety, 'What will happen if I say this?' are the biggest distractors. Or, for example, you go to a party and you find out a gentleman whom you have been trying to meet for a long time for a deal. He is surrounded by guests. Although he is the man you wanted to meet, you step back. You do not get the courage to meet him. Fear and anxiety are our second biggest distractor in improving our communication skills.

The third, of course, are our habits—'A settled or regular tendency or practice, especially one that is hard to give up.' We have built habits, good and bad, and all our communication skills and where they are today are a result of our habits. Our unwillingness to write and procrastinate are bad habits, and willingness to get out talk to people and listen to them are good habits. So we are placed somewhere in the middle of good versus bad with our communication skills. These habits are a result of the acts that we have done 'wrongly'. In the case of communication, we often do them unconsciously and sometimes consciously, for example, unwillingness to talk to people or talking to someone on the phone. The habits reflect on our verbal and non-verbal cues and tend to persist. It then becomes a part of 'how' and 'what' we communicate. Characteristics of a habit as described by Professor Wendy Wood and Professor David Neal in their article, *A New Look at Habits and the Habit-Goal Interface* are: *Efficiency (or lack of it), Lack of Awareness, Unintentionality and Uncontrollability*.[4] Therefore, when we keep on doing the same acts, right or wrong, in communi-cation, they grow up as habits. We lack *efficiency*, for example, when we procrastinating to write; *lack of awareness*, for example, when we are looking down while we talk; *unintentionality*,

---

[4] Wendy Wood and David Neil, 'A New Look at Habits and the Habit-Goal Interface' *Psychological Review, 114(4)*:843–863, (November 2007), https://www.researchgate.net/publication/5936907_A_New_Look_at_Habits_and_the_Habit-Goal_Interface (accessed on 30 May 2019).

for example, when we looking at the mobile when someone is talking; and *uncontrollability*, for example, when we talk loudly over phone while sharing your work space with others.

Another aspect that also holds us back is our severe unwillingness for 'continuous improvement'. Even after being given a feedback, we refuse to act on it and thereby change. Pressure of time, work and getting the food on the plates of the family (earning money) are some other reasons why professionals find it difficult to change. They complain about their lack of time as an explanation to this behaviour.

SELF-ASSESSMENT

You will need to assess yourself on where you are and where you want to be. This journey is rocky, but interesting and gives you a wonderful insight about what you want to do. As someone who is trying to work on his communication skills, rate yourself on a scale of 1-5, with 1 being poor and 5 being excellent. However, ensure that you are neither being moderate nor too liberal. Also take into account that you are not over-estimating your capabilities. Wherever you are on the scale, you will still have some scopes of improvement. Figure them out. You could be a poor listener or someone who is bad at drafting a message, a chronic procrastinator, a boring presenter or a person with poor conversation and negotiation skills. Once done, focus on couple of them—ideally not more than 2-3 of these areas—and start working towards that. At the end of this chapter, I will be sharing some thoughts on how you could self-improve.

The step two of this process is to understand your behaviour, especially when it comes to communicating with others.

All the questions are scaled 1-5, with 1 being poor and 5 being excellent.

1. When I speak, I use my arms, eyes and other gestures appropriately (1—2—3—4—5).

2. When talking, I make an eye contact with the other person (1—2—3—4—5).

3. I love meeting new people, within and outside my organization (1—2—3—4—5).

4. I love to know more about people whom I am meeting for the first time (1—2—3—4—5).

5. When I am conversing with people, I try to force my opinion on others (1—2—3—4—5).

6. When I am talking with others, I listen to the ideas of others (1—2—3—4—5).

7. When someone comes to meet me, I leave all my work to listen to what they have to say (1—2—3—4—5).

8. I give a genuine hearing to people (1—2—3—4—5).

9. I am comfortable to confront others (1—2—3—4—5).

10. When someone gives me a feedback, I work on it (1—2—3—4—5).

11. I spend time in preparing to present (1—2—3—4—5).

12. When I present, my objective is to reach the heart of the audience (1—2—3—4—5).

13. I am open and honest in communicating with my team (1—2—3—4—5).

14. If because of a wrong communication from my end, there is a failure, I do not mind admitting it in front of my team members (1—2—3—4—5).

15. I spend good amount of time writing, which is complete, precise and accurate (1—2—3—4—5).

16. I always pass on this job of writing to others (1—2—3—4—5).

The above questions are the eight areas of communication we have discussed. Each of these areas has two questions each: Non-verbal, networking, conversations, listening, difficult conversations, presenting, team communication and writing.

Do you see any areas you are very strong with? Have you identified areas you are weak in? How do you plan to maximize your strengths and minimize your weaknesses? From the steps one and two, how do you feel is your general level of communication? And what are the key areas you need to improve?

To do a further detailed analysis of your ability to communicate, you need to do a SWOT analysis. This is the step three of this process. List down your *strengths, weaknesses, opportunities and threats*. Remember that strengths and weaknesses are internal to you, and opportunities and threats are external to you.

Strengths: What are the areas in communication you do really well?

Weaknesses: What are the areas you need to improve in?

Opportunities: What are the opportunities available to you to strengthen your strengths and work on your weaknesses?

Threats: What are the things that are likely to prevent you from doing so?

This will help you prioritize and set a goal. Set a goal that is *SMART: Specific, measurable, achievable, realistic and time-bound*. What do you want to achieve? How will you measure it? What are the things that you intend to do to achieve your goal? Is it realistic? By when do you want to complete this?

Being realistic is the key in setting this goal sheet for yourself. A frequently asked question to me is, 'can I improve it in six months?' The answer is, 'I do not know.' This is because I do not know your schedule, where you are today, how much time can you afford to improve, what are the avenues available for you to practice and so on. You can be your best judge to answer the question. The second key aspect is continuous improvements and working consciously to achieve the goals. We often deviate from the goals we have set because we do not want/we forget about our goal of continuous and conscious improvement. Every time a person walks in to my cubicle to talk to me, I forget the goal I had set for myself, 'not to interrupt a person while talking.' Sometimes you do it, sometimes you forget. This does not work.

THE CONTINUOUS IMPROVEMENT MODEL

Continuous improvement, explained briefly, is a never-ending strive for perfection in everything you do.[5] Derived from the word *kaizen*, where 'kai' translates to change and 'zen' as for the better.[6] This method consists of three fundamental principles: *Feedback, efficiency and evolution*, which means reflection of the processes, building efficiency to the processes and taking small steps rather than giant ones.

Constant feedback is an important aspect of the model. Open communication with your team and colleagues and accepting the feedbacks given to you by your people are critical for improvement.[7]

We keep doing the same things again and again, not bothering about the processes. We talk the way we did, present the way we have been doing, avoid difficult conversations like we did, do not improve our basic processes or the way we did them or have been doing for so long. It is therefore time to relook at how we have been doing and what are the changes needed to make the process more efficient. Therefore, for communication, look at the way you have been doing it, make changes to it, implement them and review them by taking feedback.

The last concept of taking small steps is important because large changes are difficult to implement. When we make smaller changes, they do not increase our anxiety, instead reduce and improve our speed of improvement.[8]

---

[5] Wikipedia, 'Continual Improvement Process,' Wikipedia, https://en.wikipedia.org/wiki/Continual_improvement_process (accessed on 30 May 2019).

[6] Kaizen Institute, 'What Is Kaizen?' Kaizen Institute, https://www.kaizen.com/what-is-kaizen.html (accessed on 30 May 2019).

[7] Kanbanize, 'What Is Continuous Improvement? Definition & Tools,' Kanbanize, https://kanbanize.com/lean-management/improvement/what-is-continuous-improvement/ (accessed on 30 May 2019).

[8] Maggie Millard, '6 Principles of the Continuous Improvement Model,' *KaiNexus*, 4 October 2018, https://blog.kainexus.com/continuous-improvement/6-principles-of-the-continuous-improvement-model (accessed on 30 May 2019).

After you have completed your self-assessments, it is time to put it into action. Take one or two of your goals at a time. For example, if you have listed five–six things that you want to improve take only the most critical ones or the ones which require your immediate attention. This ideally should not be more than two areas. You should then do the following:

Step 1: Reflect on the areas you intend to improve and what we have been doing so far and what you want to improve upon.

Step 2: What are the changes that you want to bring in?

Step 3: Make the changes. Keep practicing.

Step 4: Take feedback and measure if you have improved or not.

Let us take an example. If you want to improve on your ability to listen well, list down things that you have been doing so far. For example, you have not been able to give time to people, you have been multi-tasking and you have been frequently interrupted by others. (Step 1)

So for all the things that you want to improve, the changes that you want to bring in are…. List them down. (Step 2)

Make the changes, but do it consciously. Take small steps at a time. The more you practice the better it is. 'Practice makes a man perfect.' (Step 3)

Take feedback and see if there are further scopes of improvement. (Step 4)

For the feedback, use the feedback mechanism of your organization. In case there is none, ask your team members to provide an anonymous feedback for you. Apart from the other parameters that you are putting in, also include the things that you wanted to improve in your ability to communicate. Do this continuously and you will be able to see the change. Reflect on the feedbacks given and try and improve on them further.

TAKING THE BABY STEPS

We all are subject to some bad habits while we communicate. We need to eliminate them and take steps to ensure that the communication we do becomes effective and efficient.

Start with couple of baby steps. For example, you could start with keeping your phone away while listening or just avoid interrupting others while they talk to you. You can also work towards improving your vocabulary. You can start by one–two words daily, which will help you at work. However, remember that business writing is different. Chose words that are simple and easy. Similarly greeting people when you meet them or smiling at people who you do not know and greeting them. For each of the areas that you have identified, work on the things that will help you improve your effectiveness.

Here is a list of items which will help you think further.

Non-verbal communication	• Be genuinely interested while talking to people. • Be genuinely interested while listening to people. • Give a smile while you are talking with others. • Greet people when you meet them. • Dress professionally for every occasion.
Networking	• Get to know at least few new people every month. • Revive your old contacts and start initiating a conversation with them. • Speak to the person whom you thought was the most difficult one.
Conversations	• Do not push your ideas on others. • Keep your mind open while conversing. • If you do not understand, clarify and summarize.
Listening	• Avoid multi-tasking. • Be interested genuinely. • Don't advise unless asked for. • Do not interrupt.
Difficult conversations	• Do not discourage people to discuss the elephant in the room. • If it needs to be spoken out, speak. • Express your feelings. • Do you respond or react?

Presenting	• Prepare for your presentations. • Rehearse. • Analyse your audience before you speak.
Communication in groups	• Be honest and open. • Ensure that you build up your trust. • Encourage others to speak up. • Empathize with your people.
Written communication	• Read to write better. Reading gives you breadth and depth as well. • Choose talking to a person over writing. • When you write be as precise as possible.

Start changing your smaller bad habits a step at a time. For example, 'replying to all' in an email unless absolutely necessary. It could be pertaining to your listening capabilities; fiddling with your pen, hair, mobile, pencil or anything around you; being a criticizer or complainer; being irrelevant; hijacking the meetings and blaming people using a negative tone. Using 'and', 'but' and 'I' is irritating. For example, 'I know this, but…' or just ramble without any substance. For example, 'I have been doing this for ages, because I am certified….' Interrupting people while they speak, not preparing for presentation, not finding out newer and effective ways to present, not willing to connect or network with people and more.

LEARN TO COMMUNICATE

Breathing is an involuntary activity: We do not have a control on how we breathe. This is not true for communication though. We have a control on how we communicate, talk to people, get our thoughts through or listen to them. However, what restricts us from doing so are our inhibitions, habits, lack of self-awareness and fear/anxieties. So the big question is can we change the way we communicate? The answer is definitely 'yes'. I believe we can. People can learn it too. In these years of working across different companies and with different people, I have seen people changing from bad to good and vice versa. But like other changes, it is not easy. It requires self-awareness, determination, guts, consistency and continuous improvement.

Virginia Satir's, family therapist, research and work provide a lot of input to the change that we have embarked upon. Virginia Satir (1972) described communication as[9]

> A huge umbrella that covers and affects all that goes on between human beings' and that all communication is learned. Satir referred to communication as 'a film camera equipped with sound ...that works only in the present, right here, right now, between you and me.

Whatever we are trying to communicate with others can only be through verbal and non-verbal mechanisms. While verbal refers to words spoken and written, non-verbal refers to neither spoken nor written communication. We can be taught verbal communication, but non-verbal is involuntary. It comes with genuine behaviour of a person. If you are honest, your body, face and speech will display honesty; if you are hiding things from others, your non-verbal's will show up.

Verbal communication is powerful yet suffers from a limit. We use it to describe our thoughts and feelings. If you say, 'I am eating my lunch', the word 'lunch' has a significance. It means different things to different people owing to the way they have been taught to interpret it from their childhood. 'For example, 'undisciplined Rama is highly' does not mean anything unless you arrange them in an order. Non-verbal communication is difficult to measure. The clothes you wear, your pitch, tone and voice, your posture and gestures and so on cannot be measured. Remember that non-verbal communication could be ambiguous, but is continuous and conveys emotions. Whether you talk or not, your jittery feeling or standing still communicates to others. It is also highly ambiguous. Scratching your head, for example, could be a result of dandruff or a sign of confusion. Both of these are very powerful, with its own limitations and it is up to you to use them for your benefit in different situations and circumstances.

---

[9] *Awaken*, 'Family Therapy and the Theories of Virginia Satir,' *Awaken*, 13 December 2015, https://www.awaken.com/2015/12/family-therapy-and-the-theories-of-virginia-satir/ (accessed on 30 May 2019).

This change can be brought only by you and for you. However, be self-aware, take a stock of things going wrong, take actions to correct them and finally get feedback to fine tune them. It is a continuous process and life-long learning. You can neither stop nor reach any heights because there will always be a new peak. Just keep learning and enjoying the experience. Do not be scared or fearful of trying things. Keep an open mind and make a change to the way you communicate.

About the Author

Dr Hory Sankar Mukerjee is currently working as Principal—Education, Training and Assessment at Infosys Ltd. He has an experience of over 16 plus years in information technology, banking and media. At Infosys he currently manages the learning and development needs of 10,000+ SAP consultants. He has been awarded the Infosys 'Awards for Excellence' for his exemplary contribution to people development.

A doctorate in marketing and an MBA, he is closely associated with academics. He has three books to his credit and numerous publications in both national and international journals. His books are taught in some of the premier institutes in India and South East Asia. He has been an invited author for some of the leading blogs and publications in India and abroad, and a speaker at various conferences.

He loves to travel, listen to music and cook.

Data talks through stories

Stories leave a powerful impact, which is not possible with data alone. Very often, teams struggle to connect the dots in understanding valuable insights behind data and have a hard time in making critical data-based decisions.

Bhawna Agarwal
CEO, Serial Entrepreneur; Advisor to VCs